Guid

VOL 23 / PART 3

Edited by **Jeremy Duff and Katharine Dell**

Suggestions for using *Guidelines*

Set aside a regular time and place, if possible, when you can read and pray undisturbed. Before you begin, take time to be still and, if you find it helpful, use the BRF prayer.

In *Guidelines*, the introductory section provides context for the passages or themes to be studied, while the units of comment can be used daily, weekly, or whatever best fits your timetable. You will need a Bible (more than one if you want to compare different translations) as Bible passages are not included. At the end of each week is a 'Guidelines' section, offering further thoughts about, or practical application of what you have been studying.

You may find it helpful to keep a journal to record your thoughts about your study, or to note items for prayer. Another way of using *Guidelines* is to meet with others to discuss the material, either regularly or occasionally.

Occasionally, you may read something in *Guidelines* that you find particularly challenging, even uncomfortable. This is inevitable in a series of notes which draws on a wide spectrum of contributors, and doesn't believe in ducking difficult issues. Indeed, we believe that *Guidelines* readers much prefer thought-provoking material to a bland diet that only confirms what they already think.

If you do disagree with a contributor, you may find it helpful to go through these three steps. First, think about why you feel uncomfortable. Perhaps this is an idea that is new to you, or you are not happy at the way something has been expressed. Or there may be something more substantial—you may feel that the writer is guilty of sweeping generalization, factual error, theological or ethical misjudgment. Second, pray that God would use this disagreement to teach you more about his word and about yourself. Third, think about what you will do as a result of the disagreement. You might resolve to find out more about the issue, or write to the contributor or the editors of *Guidelines*. After all, we aim to be 'doers of the word', not just people who hold opinions about it.

Writers in this issue

Katharine Dell is Senior Lecturer in the Faculty of Divinity at Cambridge University and Director of Studies in Theology at St Catharine's College. She is also the Old Testament Editor for *Guidelines*, and the author of *Job* in BRF's *People's Bible Commentary* series.

Andrew Gregory is Chaplain of University College, Oxford. His publications include *Four Witnesses, One Gospel?* (Grove Books, 2005) and, as editor and contributor, *The Fourfold Gospel Commentary* (SPCK, 2006).

Sarah Tillett is based at a church in the West Midlands and is a trustee and director of Tearfund UK. She is chaplain to the Church of England's Media Council Conference and has edited *Caring for Creation* for BRF (2005). Previously she was a broadcaster and writer, living in Hong Kong.

Grace Emmerson was for many years involved in Old Testament teaching in the University of Birmingham and in the Open Theological College. One of her main interests is the teaching of Hebrew and the enthusiasm that this generates for biblical study. She is the author of *Nahum to Malachi* in BRF's *People's Bible Commentary* series.

Jeremy Duff is Director of Lifelong Learning in Liverpool Diocese and Canon at Liverpool Cathedral, as well as being the New Testament Editor for *Guidelines*. His latest book, *Meeting Jesus: Human Responses to a Yearning God*, was published by SPCK in 2006.

James Aitken is Teaching Fellow in Hebrew and Aramaic at the Faculty of Oriental Studies, University of Cambridge. He works on biblical languages and biblical interpretation, including Jewish interpretation and history.

Rosemary Dymond has spent the last three years as curate at the Anglican church in The Hague. Before ordination she worked as a research scientist in Leipzig, developing methods for functional brain imaging using MRI.

Paula Gooder teaches Biblical studies, both Old and New Testament, at the Queen's Ecumenical Theological Foundation, Birmingham, as well as working freelance as a biblical studies writer and lecturer. She is the author of *Hosea to Micah* in BRF's *People's Bible Commentary* series.

Further BRF reading for this issue

For more in-depth coverage of some of the passages in these Bible reading notes, we recommend the following titles.

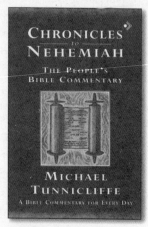

CHRONICLES *to* **NEHEMIAH**

THE PEOPLE'S BIBLE COMMENTARY

MICHAEL TUNNICLIFFE

A BIBLE COMMENTARY FOR EVERY DAY

978 1 84101 070 0, £7.99

EPHESIANS *to* **COLOSSIANS** *and* **PHILEMON**

THE PEOPLE'S BIBLE COMMENTARY

MARCUS MAXWELL

A BIBLE COMMENTARY FOR EVERY DAY

978 1 84101 047 2, £7.99

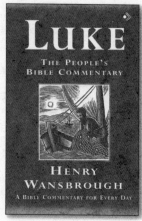

LUKE

THE PEOPLE'S BIBLE COMMENTARY

HENRY WANSBROUGH

A BIBLE COMMENTARY FOR EVERY DAY

978 1 84101 027 4, £7.99

JOSHUA *and* **JUDGES**

THE PEOPLE'S BIBLE COMMENTARY

STEVEN D. MATHEWSON

A BIBLE COMMENTARY FOR EVERY DAY

978 1 84101 095 3, £7.99

The Editors write...

A fresh perspective is a good thing; it is too easy always to see things from one point of view, whether in life in general or in our reading of the Bible. Many of the contributions in this issue challenge our perspective.

Two key characters are covered—a man and a woman. The man is the great King Solomon, known for his wisdom and his lavish wealth, and ruler during a golden age for the Israelite monarchy. The woman is Ruth, a loyal, obedient woman and a foreigner who nevertheless turns out to be the great-grandmother of King David. These characters contrast in almost every possible way, yet they are both part of the same story. Both of these contributions are from our Old Testament editor, Katharine Dell.

These character studies sandwich our continuing study of Luke's Gospel in the hands of Andrew Gregory, where we see Jesus on his journey to Jerusalem, challenging many of the views of his hearers. Then Sarah Tillett, a new contributor and director of Tearfund, leads us in a study of 'earth keeping', challenging our perspective towards God's creation. After this, Grace Emmerson, covers 2 Chronicles for us, a book presenting the history of the kings of Israel and Judah in a different light from the better-known books of Kings. Then, with our New Testament

editor Jeremy Duff, we study Paul's letter to the Colossians, which has at its heart the call to set our minds on 'things that are above', to adopt a different perspective. This is followed by Judges 1—8, featuring another new contributor, James Aitken, who teaches in the Oriental Institute in Cambridge.

Finally we reach Advent, Christmas and New Year. We try to find a new perspective on Advent and Christmas by putting extracts from hymns and poems alongside our readings. Many have enjoyed this approach of Rosemary Dymond in previous issues. Then another regular contributor, Paula Gooder, gives us some fresh thoughts on New Year from an Old Testament angle by using some psalms traditionally thought to have been used at a New Year festival held annually in ancient Israel.

We hope that this issue will help you gain a fresh perspective on the 'faith once for all entrusted to the saints' (Jude 3) which will enrich your discipleship, service and walk with God.

Katharine Dell, Jeremy Duff

The BRF Prayer

Almighty God,
you have taught us that your word is a lamp for our
feet and a light for our path. Help us, and all who
prayerfully read your word, to deepen our fellowship
with each other through your love. And in so doing
may we come to know you more fully, love you more
truly, and follow more faithfully in the steps of your
son Jesus Christ, who lives and reigns with you and
the Holy Spirit, one God for evermore. Amen.

A Prayer for Remembrance

Heavenly Father, we commit ourselves to work in
penitence and faith for reconciliation between the
nations, that all people may, together, live in
freedom, justice and peace. We pray for all who in
bereavement, disability and pain continue to suffer
the consequences of fighting and terror. We
remember with thanksgiving and sorrow those whose
lives, in world wars and conflicts past and present,
have been given and taken away.

FROM AN ORDER OF SERVICE FOR REMEMBRANCE SUNDAY,
CHURCHES TOGETHER IN BRITAIN AND IRELAND 2005

KING SOLOMON

The character of Solomon is in many ways an idealized figure: his crowning achievement is the building of the Jerusalem temple, he is filled with the gift of wisdom, he enjoys the fruits of his father David's military exploits in governing over a prosperous and sizeable united kingdom, and he is wealthy beyond measure. No king is perfect, but by comparison to most of the other Davidic kings, Solomon is quite a role model. The Deutero-nomists who put together the history from Joshua through to 2 Kings clearly had a positive opinion of Solomon and, in most of the passages we will be considering, this positive assessment comes through, yet there is the occasional note of criticism and recognition of errors made. We will also cross-refer at times to the Chronicler's account of the reign, which is even more positive, especially in regard to the temple building which is at the centre of the Chronicler's post-exilic concerns.

The version of the Bible that I shall be quoting is the NRSV.

1 The struggle over the accession

1 Kings 1:11–27

At the beginning of 1 Kings, King David is an elderly man and possibly no longer fully in control of what is going on in his kingdom. Notably, his son Adonijah plots behind his back to become king after him, building up a small army and getting some powerful figures on his side, such as Joab the military commander and Abiathar the priest. Adonijah makes a very public sacrifice in 1 Kings 1:9–10, but we are told that 'he did not invite the prophet Nathan or Benaiah or the warriors or his brother Solomon'.

We join this situation at verse 11, when Nathan teams up with Bath-sheba, Solomon's mother, to promote Solomon's claim to the throne. Nathan concocts a plan whereby Bathsheba will first approach the king on the matter and then Nathan will back her up. This is perhaps surprising, given Nathan's opposition to David's original affair with Bathsheba in

2 Samuel 12. It is a life-and-death matter, however, for if Adonijah were to become king he would surely dispose of any possible rivals to his throne.

On Nathan's instruction, Bathsheba reminds David of his promise to make Solomon his successor. This is the first we have heard of such a promise, and we cannot help wondering whether there is a form of autosuggestion going on here, taking advantage of David's elderly state to 'remind' him of a promise he hasn't actually made. Alternatively, of course, in less cynical vein, such a promise might have been made but not recorded in the Deuteronomic history. Bathsheba then reveals that Adonijah has become king already—even while David himself is alive! This is a real challenge to David's authority. She emphasizes that it is indeed David's decision as to who will follow him on the throne, and reminds him of the danger to herself and her son if Adonijah is crowned after David's death. Nathan re-emphasizes the challenge to David's authority by those who proclaimed the royal acclamation, 'Long live King Adonijah!' in the festivities after the sacrifice. We are now poised to hear David's reaction.

The first two chapters of 1 Kings form the end of what is known as the 'succession narrative'. Succession is the main theme of this sophisticated literary narrative, which includes the preceding attempt of Absalom to usurp David's throne. This section of the Deuteronomistic history is thought to have a quite individual character. There is little mention of God—he is very much behind the scenes rather than being shown actively involved in events—and the concerns are quite political. The text may have started as a court narrative about the succession, which was later incorporated into the Deuteronomistic history by its authors. It may have been penned by scribes from the court of Solomon himself, writing up the history of the accession to favour Solomon. In that connection, it may be linked to the Wisdom enterprise promoted by such scribes.

2 Solomon becomes king

1 Kings 1:28—40

David acts quickly to rectify the situation. He assures Bathsheba that Solomon shall succeed him and that, indeed, he will start to rule during

David's declining years. This section seems to suggest that Bathsheba and Nathan are no longer in the king's presence and that they have to be summoned afresh (see vv. 28, 32): maybe we have some disjunction in the sources here. Nathan the prophet, Zadok the priest and Benaiah take Solomon down to Gihon, where there is a spring (mentioned in 2 Chronicles 32:30 as part of the Hezekiah tunnel complex). Solomon rides on David's mule in order to be anointed king there (compare Psalm 110, a psalm of royal accession). This might remind us of the time when Jesus rode by donkey into Jerusalem from the Mount of Olives (Matthew 21:5): are there deliberate overtones of this kingly anointing from the Old Testament in the New Testament account?

David authorizes Solomon to sit on his throne, to rule in his place (v. 35), which probably denotes some kind of co-regency. Zadok and Nathan follow David's commands, as loyal servants should, and Benaiah even offers the prayer that Solomon's reign might be greater than that of David. Again the Lord is behind the scenes, often invoked in prayer, while the action is by human instigation. The trio seems, in verse 38, to be joined by the Pelethites (an unknown group) and the Cherethites (possibly a Cretan group of Philistines). The people follow the lead of their priests and prophets and proclaim Solomon king.

If you go on reading, you will find Adonijah's panicked reaction to these events, his supporters' desertion of him and Solomon's gracious sparing of his life (later overturned when Adonijah starts to make requests that Solomon finds threatening: see 2:13–25). It is interesting that none of this information about the rivalry for the throne is contained in the Chronicler's account. If we turn to 1 Chronicles 28, we find Solomon announced by David as his successor—but in the context of temple building. In verse 7 God promises to establish Solomon's kingdom for ever if he continues to keep God's commandments, and this is another of the Chronicler's themes—reward for good deeds and punishment for wickedness. When, in 1 Chronicles 29:22b, Solomon is anointed king, all the leaders, warriors and sons of David pledge allegiance to him. In the Chronicler's rather idealistic world, written with the hindsight of a number of centuries, the warring and politicking about which we read in 1 Kings is all omitted. Some stories he does repeat in full, but he is unashamedly selective in what he chooses to present. Kings and Chronicles are both 'histories' of Israel and yet we see, particularly with the Chronicler, that we might need to take the word 'history' with a large pinch of salt.

3 Solomon's wisdom

1 Kings 3:1–15

1 Kings 2 starts to form an impression of Solomon's fairness as he deals with his opponents and gives them extra chances, but in chapter 3 his wisdom is confirmed. He first makes a political marriage with the Egyptian Pharaoh's daughter (unnamed, as many women are in the Old Testament). We are also told that Solomon loved the Lord—an expression of his loyalty—and that he is walking in the statutes of his father, which is the Deuteronomist's seal of approval. We are informed briefly of his building work: the palace had to be completed, as well as the temple and wall around Jerusalem. The central sanctuary at Jerusalem was to be of key importance in preventing the fragmentation of worship throughout the country. Much of this worship was done at the 'high places' mentioned in verse 2, which were former Canaanite shrines where it was difficult to monitor pure Yahwistic practice. Having said that, we are told in verses 3–4 that Solomon made somewhat excessive sacrificial offerings at high places, notably at Gibeon. It is possible that these large numbers have an air of the legendary, or at least of an account that has grown in the telling.

It is there at Gibeon that he has a dream in which he asks the Lord for the discernment to rule well. In this account, Solomon reveals his youth and inexperience: it sounds as if he is overawed by the great things that the Lord did for his father David and by the great size of the nation that he is now to rule over. He asks God therefore for 'an understanding mind to govern your people, able to discern between good and evil' (v. 9). This request goes down well with God, who is impressed that Solomon asked neither for wealth nor for success over his enemies. He grants his request, giving Solomon 'a wise and discerning mind' (v. 12), and, since Solomon did not ask, he gives him riches too (the usual product of wisdom) and longevity (another great blessing in Hebrew thought)—subject to good behaviour, of course!

When Solomon awakes from the dream, perhaps we are left to wonder whether it is going to come true: that has yet to be proven. In a way, the dream is a legitimation of his earlier succession as an unproven youth: now his wisdom and sagacity are God-given. In the meantime, he makes another sacrifice—this time before the ark in Jerusalem—just for good measure.

4 Solomon's judgment

1 Kings 3:16–28

Solomon is accredited elsewhere in the Old Testament with the writing of Proverbs (see 1:1; 10:1) and with the authorship of Ecclesiastes (the author is described there as 'son of David, king in Jerusalem' (1:1). He is also mentioned as the author of the very late apocryphal book, the Wisdom of Solomon. This endowment of wisdom makes him the figurehead and hero of 'the wise', a group of sages who probably worked at the royal court in administrative, political and literary roles and who supported the large state that emerged under Solomon. We know of the existence of sages in neighbouring Egypt. Egypt was the real centre of wisdom at the time and we have many instructions and other documents still extant that are the products of that genre. Babylon too had its wisdom tradition, inherited from the Sumerians. A wisdom tradition seems to have been an international enterprise, and it is likely that a similar system flourished in Israel at this time, with Solomon at its head as the wise man *par excellence*.

In this passage we are given an example of Solomon's exercise of his God-given wisdom—proof, if you like, of the truth of God's words in the dream. Solomon's task is to solve an argument between two women, described as prostitutes, over whose is the living baby. It is interesting that one of the king's roles is as a judge in a public assembly and that the women in this story appear to have direct access to him. Wisdom, as presented in Proverbs, involves moral discernment between righteous and unrighteous thoughts and deeds. This example, the only one given us of Solomon's prowess in wisdom, demonstrates the kind of insight into human nature required to make such a moral discernment. When Solomon proclaims that he has discovered the true mother of the child, his execution of justice stuns the people by its wisdom. It is worth noting that wisdom often involves a little guile!

11

5 Wealth, material and spiritual

1 Kings 4:20–34

Verse 20 shows a vision of the contentment and prosperity of the united kingdoms of Judah and Israel, indicated by the great number of people making up the nation. In the statement that they 'ate and drank and were happy', there is an echo of the advice that Ecclesiastes 8:15 offers to eat and drink and enjoy the life God has given. The immensity of the food provision for Solomon and his entourage, just for one day (vv. 22–23), is another demonstration of his wealth. He also has economic power over neighbouring states (including Israel's old enemies, the Philistines, who pay tribute to Solomon to show their vassalage to him, v. 21) and is enjoying peaceful relations with them. The name Solomon is related semantically to the word *shalom*, meaning 'peace'. We are given details of Solomon's chariots and horsemen, giving an indication of his considerable military might. Nothing was lacking materially and Solomon was able to be generous.

In verse 29 we return to Solomon's wisdom, which is described as 'vast as the sand on the seashore'. Egypt is mentioned here for its wisdom, as are the people of the east—possibly a reference to Babylon or even to Persia. Particularly wise individuals are named in verse 31, but we know no further details about them. Then comes a link with proverbs, in the detail that Solomon composed three thousand of them (many more than appear in the biblical book of Proverbs). There may be some exaggeration in the round numbers here. Songs are also mentioned—and, of course, another traditional attribution to Solomon is the Song of Songs (or Song of Solomon), which is about love between a man and a woman. Jewish tradition relates that Solomon composed the Song of Songs in his youth, Proverbs in middle age and Ecclesiastes when he was old and grey.

Finally we learn that Solomon had an encyclopaedic knowledge of the natural world, of fish and animals, birds and reptiles, such that people would flock to hear him speak. We know a type of catalogue, from Egypt, called *onomastica*, used in educational contexts, in which varieties of species are listed, so maybe there is a parallel with Solomon's knowledge here.

2 Chronicles 1 gives us a very abbreviated account of Solomon's military and commercial activity that varies quite considerably from the 1 Kings account, and there is no further description of his wisdom.

6 Solomon builds the temple

1 Kings 6:1–22

The climax of Solomon's reign is the building of the temple, and the Deuteronomists pause on this issue for several chapters, beginning in chapter 5 with the preparations and ending in chapter 8 with the dedication of the temple. The building of Solomon's palace is also described in chapter 7, but in much less detail than the description of the temple.

Chapter 6 opens rather grandly, with the exact date for the start of the building and the measurement of lengths, depths and heights in cubits. (The NIV helpfully provides equivalent measurements in feet and metres.) There is a vestibule as well as the main house, and there is an outer area as well as an inner sanctuary. The roof is finished off in cedar, a most expensive wood. The impression of the whole building is one of grandeur and size, and of no expense spared.

In verses 11–12 we find a repetition of the promise to Solomon that first appeared in chapter 3, with attendant conditional clauses about good behaviour. God also states his intention to dwell in this temple among the people, and declares his loyalty to all of them. The concept of God's actual presence in the temple in Jerusalem, once the ark is housed there, is well attested in the Old Testament.

The details of the interior show that both cedar wood and cypress wood are used. The inner sanctuary—all cedar, with carvings—would house the ark of the covenant in which were contained the most holy tablets of stone, the Ten Commandments. Gold is then added to the picture: gold in excess, not just in the sanctuary but over the whole house. The description continues to the end of the chapter, with details of all the temple furnishings, the carvings of cherubim, the doors and so on, until its completion seven years later (v. 38). This description seems elaborate and detailed enough, but the Chronicler goes further: in 2 Chronicles 3 the building commences, in chapter 4 the furnishings are described, in chapter 5 the ark arrives and the temple is dedicated in chapter 6. The Chronicler gives this even greater emphasis because in post-exilic times, when he was writing (in the absence of a monarchy and of a political state), the temple was more at the heart of life than ever before. Interestingly, too, the Chronicler plays down the building work that Solomon does for himself, such as his palace—all is shown to be for the glory of the Lord.

Guidelines

The strongest theme that comes across to us from these chapters is the importance of wisdom. It is seen as God-given, and it encompasses understanding, skill, discernment, tact, good communication, sound judgment, the ability to lead and to rule if necessary, diplomacy, literary artistry and solid knowledge. What a range of abilities, for which we also might pray! Sound wisdom leads to all good things, and there is a traditional nexus between wisdom and wealth. Of course, this doesn't always follow—there are wealthy fools and very poor wise people—but the message is that conscientious behaviour in all areas of life leads to success, to the respect of others, to being given opportunities, authority over others and the chance of leadership. From these things, sometimes, material rewards also flow.

Wisdom is about being on the right track. The book of Proverbs often likens life to a path, and the choice is ours. We can choose the rutted path covered in thorns if we are foolish enough to do so, but the preferred course is the smooth path on which one set of choices opens further doors of opportunity. God directs the steps of the person on this path, although human beings might think that they are making immediate decisions about their direction: it is a subtle interplay between human action and divine ordering.

Solomon, then, had the gift of wisdom in abundance—God-given, as we might recognize all gifts to be. Let us end this reflection on wisdom with Reinhold Niebuhr's 'serenity prayer':

God grant me the serenity to accept the things I cannot change; courage to change the things I can; and the wisdom to know the difference.

1 Solomon's palace

1 Kings 7:1–12; 10:14–22

Unlike the Chronicler, the Deuteronomists are interested in the details of Solomon's palace. He took longer to build it than he did the temple—13 years as opposed to seven. Perhaps the delay was because he was focusing on the temple, or maybe there is a hint that he took even more care over his own house (compare the complaints of the prophet in Haggai 1:4–9). Once again we read details of measurements and the extensive use of cedar. The cedars of Lebanon were the best to be found and were widely famed; hence the description of Solomon's palace as the house of the Forest of Lebanon. Solomon makes his own residential quarters and then a similar set of quarters for his Egyptian bride. Costly stones are used: no expense is spared.

Lavish provision of gold is not mentioned in chapter 7, which suggests that Solomon has shown restraint in his own palace, but chapter 10 gives us more detail. Huge amounts of gold are seen to come in from all the trading posts around the region for Solomon to use for his own purposes. (Again, NIV gives modern equivalents for the quantities described.) He thus makes shields for his house, and a throne of ivory overlaid with gold, with a footstool of gold and statues of lions in attendance. Solomon's drinking vessels were also made of gold: silver simply wasn't rated!

2 Solomon's prayer of dedication

1 Kings 8:22–30

Much is made of the actual dedication of the temple. The account begins at the start of chapter 8, as the elders are summoned to attend, the ark is brought up to Jerusalem, and the glory of the Lord arrives in thick cloud. Solomon makes a speech about the history behind the building of the temple, which is followed in our passage by his prayer of dedication. This prayer is sometimes regarded by scholars as having been compiled by the Deuteronomists rather than being the verbatim words of Solomon himself. Historically, Solomon would no doubt have said something along these lines, but we have ancient historians acting as our guides.

Solomon's prayer is a eulogy to God's greatness, echoing the Ten Commandments in the words that 'there is no God like you', and recalling the covenant-making with David. The prayer for a continued Davidic line is reiterated, and then there is a moment of humility as Solomon reflects on God's greatness. This mere temple cannot contain such a one, yet he prays that God may indeed dwell there and listen to the prayers of his people in that holy place. In like manner, all synagogues, churches and other places of worship, although they may not lay claim to any physical signs of God's presence, are dedicated in the same way, in that God is asked to listen to the prayers of his people within these structures and to dwell in such places in a more profound way than in the world at large. This is a reminder to us of the nature of any 'holy place', this temple being the 'holy of holies'. When we think of the Wailing Wall, the only last vestige of Solomon's temple, and the way in which it is venerated today, it gives us a glimpse of the significance that the whole construction must have had.

The Chronicler echoes the prayer of dedication in 2 Chronicles 6:12–21, which fits in with his assessment of the significance of the temple in the life of the newly restored post-exilic community.

3 Promise and threat

1 Kings 9:1–9

Despite the very positive assessment of Solomon's reign that we have read so far, there is, lurking in the background, an element of conditionality. Even the continuance of David's line through Solomon is seen to be contingent on good behaviour. This moral aspect is drawn out particularly in chapter 9 and serves as a reminder that all these blessings are not to be taken for granted. It is easy for the wealthy and successful to forget their duties to others or their gratitude for help offered along the way. Solomon might have forgotten that all this success was in the gift of God alone.

In this passage God makes a second appearance to Solomon in a dream and confirms that he has heard Solomon's prayer. He is pleased with the house that has been built for him and promises to dwell there for ever. The words 'eyes' and 'heart' in relation to God are unusual in their anthropomorphism, but they express the idea that God is seeing all that is there and that his innermost emotions are involved.

God confirms his establishment of Solomon's throne, as long as Solomon remains full of 'integrity' and 'uprightness' (v. 4). There is no suggestion here that the king will diverge from an upright path, but a reminder of the threat is still given, which is then expanded in verses 6–9. These verses may be a later addition, made with hindsight, as we know that many of the kings of Israel and Judah did diverge from the path of integrity and worshipped other gods. They have perhaps been inserted by the Deuteronomists as a warning to those who came later, and as a kind of justification for the calamities that were to come about at the time of the fall of the northern and southern kingdoms, many centuries hence. The Deuteronomists are known to have added such passages of warning (for example, see the exhortations in Joshua 1 and 23) at key turning points in the life of the nation.

The major threat seen in this passage is the worship of other gods (v. 6), a topic that we have not encountered before in this section and which seems out of place in this grand positive narrative about the temple. We have to remember, however, that it was not many years before the temple was polluted with the idols of false gods. It is a sad indictment upon the house of Israel that they could not sustain the loyalty and integrity shown by Solomon and his father before him. The Chronicler echoes this chapter in 2 Chronicles 7:12–22. For him, the indictment is a justification of the exile through which his people have come. For them, there is no longer a house of David—all the grand promises of a continuing dynasty came to nought—but the temple has been rebuilt, and that remains the focus of the Chronicler's hope for the present and the future.

4 The queen of Sheba

1 Kings 10:1–13

We are now introduced to the queen of Sheba, who comes to test King Solomon 'with hard questions'. She was probably on a trade mission, although this is not the way the text presents the visit. Sheba was in the east, the traditional home of wisdom, and was possibly the Sabean empire: Sabeans are mentioned in Job 1:15 and Sheba in Genesis 25:1–6. The queen of Sheba too is wealthy, and she is very much Solomon's equal intellectually. Solomon successfully answers all of her questions and so passes her test. Interestingly we are in the realm of riddles and wordplay here, a different form of wisdom from the proverbs and listings described in 1 Kings 5 and the administrative skill demonstrated in 1 Kings 3.

The queen is impressed by Solomon's wisdom and by his temple and the opulence all around: she might not have expected much from a small state like Israel. She expresses to him that he has far exceeded her expectation and she blesses God's choice of king. She gives him gold from Ophir, spices and precious stones and almug wood (a fine wood, but not known as to precise type) as well as musical instruments of various types. In return he grants her every desire (we are given no detail…) and return gifts. Her visit seems mainly to underline Solomon's wealth, power, wisdom and beneficence.

The Chronicler echoes the Deuteronomistic account almost word for word in 2 Chronicles 9. Handel immortalized the visit in his piece 'The arrival of the queen of Sheba'. Such compositions, which have made certain biblical passages famous, are an important part of the history of interpretation of the Bible. Music, art and literature all combine to provide us with a rich picture of how past generations have appreciated these biblical passages.

5 Solomon's errors

1 Kings 11:1–13

We come now to a passage which is the first real cloud on the horizon, as we are told of Solomon's penchant for foreign women. These women come from nations prohibited by God for intermarriage on the grounds of the possibility of apostasy. However, Solomon keeps going down this path. Nehemiah has something to say on this issue when he criticizes Hebrews for marrying foreign wives and cites Solomon in that context (Nehemiah 13:23–27), but the Chronicler omits this criticism of Solomon entirely. As the great temple builder, Solomon is one of his heroes and so, for the Chronicler, he is above criticism.

We are told that Solomon had 700 princess brides and 300 concubines, which seems an excessive number for anyone! It reminds us, perhaps, of his rather overextravagant sacrificing at Gibeon and other high places: everything Solomon does, he does on a grand scale. Alternatively, maybe these stories grew in the telling.

Solomon's wives influenced him, in his old age, to go after other gods, notably Astarte, famous goddess of the Sidonians (also the Canaanites), and Milcom, god of the Ammonites. This is the first sign of evil deeds committed by Solomon, but he then goes further and builds a high place for Chemosh, the Moabite god (v. 7). This is enough to elicit God's anger, and from this comes the threat to divide the kingdom so that Solomon's descendants will rule over only one part of it. That part was to be Judah, the southern kingdom, which for much of the century that followed was the less powerful of the two kingdoms.

This is a sad ending to the tale of Solomon's wisdom, wealth and success, and it shows that all are fallible, even the great, such as he. Perhaps it sounds a note of realism in an otherwise overoptimistic account. Needless to say, none of it is mentioned by the Chronicler.

6 Greatness and death

1 Kings 10:23–29; 11:41–3

A rewind of the tape takes us back into chapter 10, back to the positive picture of Solomon with which I would like to end. His riches and wisdom (note, in that order) are mentioned in verse 23. His popularity is emphasized, as well as the God-given nature of his powers of wisdom. When people came from far and wide, each brought a present: he must have been like a member of our royal family today, with gifts in abundance from all around the known world. We are given an insight into his chariotry and horses, and we have a reference to the commonness of silver—not here (as in 2 Chronicles 9:20) that it was not a valuable metal in those days, but rather that it was so common in Solomon's Jerusalem that it was not worthy of note. Precious cedars, too, were so numerous that they were like sycamores. Egypt was known for its powerful horses (see Isaiah 30:15), and Kue is thought to have been a horse-breeding area, so it is hardly surprising that Solomon bought them from there. He also acted as a point of export of goods to other nations.

We turn finally to the death of Solomon. There was clearly a book called the Book of the Acts of Solomon, which existed at this time of writing but is now lost to us. It may be that this was a source for both Deuteronomists and Chronicler. This is true, too, in relation to 'The Books of the Annals of the Kings' that the Deuteronomist also mentions (see 2 Kings 21:17). We have to hope that there is not much missing from the account in Kings that the Deuteronomist thought could be read elsewhere and so wasn't worth including! We shall never know the answer to that question, however. This section is probably a Deuteronomic composition, as are so many of the summaries of the reigns of kings in this long history.

Solomon gets a good verdict: he had a long and prosperous reign and he was given a good burial in Jerusalem with his father David. His son, Rehoboam, succeeded him.

Guidelines

In the book of Ecclesiastes, ostensibly written by 'the son of David'—this same Solomon—there is a section often called the 'Solomonic experiment', in which the king tests the various means to satisfaction to see if they fulfil his desires. One of these means is wisdom, another is pleasure, and there is also wealth. The more negative side of wisdom is brought out in this experiment—the idea that a human being can go on searching and never achieve a satisfactory resolution (Ecclesiastes 1:17–18). There we see the endlessness of the quest, and also the fact that knowledge can lead to negative as well as positive results. We might think, in modern terms, of the great strides made in many areas of scientific discovery, and yet the vexation of having invented the nuclear bomb that could destroy all that we cherish. Self-indulgent pleasure-seeking is also seen as futile (Ecclesiastes 2:1–9): wine is mentioned as a fleeting pleasure. Doing great works and having the wealth to furnish 'the lifestyle' are also seen to have their limitations.

The message is that the search was fun for a time: the king became great in wealth and wisdom and was able to have all that he desired. These chapters from Ecclesiastes, which run somewhat counter to the passages we have been considering these last two weeks, might lead us to reflect on whether wisdom, grand works, great wealth and all that our hearts desire will really lead us to happiness. In today's world, we get the impression sometimes that wealth is the key that leads to other happiness, but is it a deep and lasting satisfaction, or is there a vanity in the whole enterprise that might lead to ultimate dissatisfaction with life? The question remains open, and we may be wise to seek more to life than a surface satisfaction with material goods. True wisdom resides with God and is a gift from him.

FURTHER READING

W. Brueggemann, 'Solomon as patron of wisdom' in *The Sage in Israel and the Ancient Near East*, J.G. Gammie and L.G. Perdue (eds.), Eisenbrauns, 1990, pp. 117–32.

J. Gray, *1 and 2 Kings* (Old Testament Library), SCM Press, 1964.

Iain Provan, *1 and 2 Kings* (Old Testament Guides), Sheffield Academic Press, 1997.

LUKE 9:51—19:27

In the first part of our reading of Luke's 'orderly account' (1:3) we read the opening chapters of his Gospel. They fell in two parts: three chapters preparing for the public ministry of Jesus, and almost six chapters on his public ministry in Galilee. Here we take up Luke's Gospel again at the point at which Jesus sets his face to travel from Galilee to Jerusalem. This central section, running from 9:51 to 19:27, accounts for ten chapters or about two-fifths of the Gospel. This is significant. Luke shares with Mark (almost certainly a major source of his work: see 1:1, where Luke refers to his predecessors) and with Matthew a biographical account of Jesus' ministry that begins in Galilee, ends in Jerusalem and therefore needs Jesus to move from one to the other. But whereas Mark and Matthew each provides a relatively short account of this journey (Mark 10; Matthew 19—20), Luke devotes much more space to it. Thus he passes over Jesus' movement into the region of Tyre and Sidon (compare Mark 7:24–30; Matthew 15:21–28) and concentrates instead on one decisive journey from Galilee to Jerusalem.

At the same time, he reduces the role that Galilee plays in his account. Whereas Mark has eight chapters devoted to what Jesus did in Galilee and Matthew has 15, Luke has only six. Certainly he includes in his travel narrative much of the material that Mark and Matthew included in their accounts of Jesus' Galilean ministry, but by putting it here Luke emphasizes not that Jesus is in Galilee but that he is on his way to Jerusalem. Thus the structure of his orderly account and the theological vision that Luke sets out to present are intertwined. Luke structures his Gospel in such a way as to focus attention on Jesus' journey to Jerusalem, for it is there that the Gospel—the first of his two volumes—will reach its climax.

One of the most striking points about this section of the Gospel is the disjunction between its form and its content. Although Luke frequently reminds his readers that Jesus is on his way to Jerusalem (see 9:51, 53; 13:33; 17:11; 18:31; 19:11, 28), most of the material that he includes has nothing to do with a journey. It consists instead mainly of teaching that Jesus gives, so references to a journey are little more than pegs on which to hang this material. This reminds us that Luke presents his material according to the purposes for which he writes. He is less interested in telling us the order in which Jesus did or said things than in presenting Jesus' significance to those who will encounter him through his Gospel.

Two main themes appear to be dominant in this part of the Gospel. One is concerned to show us who Jesus is and what is the ongoing significance of his life and teaching. Jesus is making for Jerusalem in order to be taken up (9:51; compare 9:22, 31) so the divinely ordained goal towards which he moves is his ascension, which Jesus will reach only through his passion, death and resurrection. The other theme is concerned to show Jesus' teaching for the Church, which will continue to proclaim the good news that he entrusts to them. As he journeys, Jesus gives instructions to his disciples for the period from his departure until his return at the end of time.

Matthew put much of Jesus' teaching into five great sermons that helped to develop his presentation of Jesus as a new Moses, but in so doing he may have slowed down the pace of his narrative. Luke's decision to concentrate so much of Jesus' teaching into his account of Jesus' journey helps to sustain the pace of the Gospel and to carry its readers forward to Jerusalem, the only place where a prophet may be killed (13:33). As we shall see, a significant amount of Jesus' teaching that Luke presents in his travel narrative is recorded only in his Gospel.

1 Fulfilment of God's plan

Luke 9:51–62

At the beginning of his Gospel, Luke describes the events that he sets out to record as those 'that have been fulfilled among us'. He makes a similar point again as Jesus begins his journey to Jerusalem. The words that the NRSV translates 'when the days drew near' (v. 51; compare NIV, 'as the time approached') might be translated more literally 'when the days were fulfilled'. This is an expression that Luke uses to mark important transitional points in his narrative and to remind his audience that God's purposes determine the course of the events that he is narrating. Jesus does not happen to go to Jerusalem; he goes there according to and in fulfilment of the plan of God.

Most of Luke's earliest audience would have heard the Gospel read aloud in long sections. Therefore, those who heard this passage would have had still ringing in their ears both Jesus' words about the fate that he will meet when rejected by the Jerusalem-based chief priests and their allies (9:22) and Luke's reference to what Moses and Elijah said about the departure that Jesus would accomplish in Jerusalem (9:31). This is the context in which we read that Jesus 'set his face' to go to that city (v. 51). Jesus is in no doubt about what he will meet in Jerusalem, but he is obedient to his Father's will. Jesus goes and his disciples accompany him along the way (v. 57), just as disciples must follow Jesus on the way of the cross today (9:23). We must look forward and not look back (v. 62).

The ultimate goal of Jesus' journey is significant. He is going to Jerusalem in order 'to be taken up' (v. 51). Many Christians today make little of the ascension, not least since Ascension Day falls on a Thursday and is therefore often neglected in our churches. Yet here Luke emphasizes that Jesus goes to Jerusalem in order to be taken up. We are reminded that the reason we do not see Jesus for ourselves is that he has been taken up into heaven, where he is enthroned with God and intercedes for us. One who bears a body like ours, albeit made glorious at his resurrection, has gone where we shall go. One day he shall return (Acts 1:11). For now, however, one who has lived our human life and has overcome our human death reigns in heaven, from where he pours out the Spirit on his Church (Acts 2:33).

2 Workers for the harvest

Luke 10:1–24

Earlier Jesus sent out the twelve apostles (9:1–6). Now, in an account given only by Luke, he also sends out 70 (or 72: each number appears in some manuscripts, and it is difficult to determine which is more likely to be the original reading). The sending of the 70 can be read both as an account of something that took place as Jesus journeyed to Jerusalem and as a reminder of the continuity between the mission of the earthly Jesus and those who accompanied him and the mission of the later Church, which speaks and acts in his name. Already Jesus is entrusting his work to a wider circle than just the twelve apostles; already he is calling on that wider circle to ask God to send yet more workers to the plentiful harvest that awaits them (v. 2).

The 70 are simply referred to as 'others' in distinction from some of those who have gone before, perhaps those who were not willing to follow Jesus without first attending to other matters (9:59–62). If there is any significance in the fact that they are given no particular title, it may be to remind us that all who hear the Gospel according to Luke are to be doers of the word of Jesus that it contains, and that we too must work to bring in God's harvest before the crop is spoilt. We are to go and we are to pray, although Jesus' later words about disciples needing to take material provisions with them remind us that we cannot transfer every detail from this story of the 70 to the situations in which we find ourselves today (v. 4; compare 22:35–36).

Not all receive those whom Jesus sends (vv. 10–17), yet this does not detract from the joy of those who have seen demons submit to them (v. 17) or from the significance of what they have done (v. 18). Even amid opposition and a divided response to Jesus' message, the kingdom of God is advancing (v. 9) and Satan's position is weakened. What should give Jesus' disciples most joy is the assurance that their names are written in heaven (v. 20), and that we have been given to see and hear what many others do not—that in Jesus we see what God is like (vv. 21–24). As Michael Ramsay, a former Archbishop of Canterbury, has observed, 'God is Christlike and in him is no un-Christlikeness at all'.

3 Loving God and neighbour

Luke 10:25–42

Today's passage contains three distinct elements, but it is difficult to know to what extent each component helps to interpret the others. This is a question that arises constantly as we read this central section of Luke's Gospel. Certainly the lawyer's statement that those who would inherit eternal life must love their neighbour as themselves (v. 27) leads to the question that Jesus answers by the parable of the good Samaritan. Thus Luke draws connections between some teaching found also in Matthew and in Mark (vv. 25–28) and in a parable that only he records (vv. 29–37), although he has Jesus challenge the understanding of 'neighbour' that the lawyer assumes. For the lawyer, a hostile figure whose interest is to test Jesus (v. 25; see 7:30), a neighbour is someone whom he is required by the Law to love (v. 27). For Jesus, a neighbour is someone who gives love—expressed in practical and material terms that are appropriate to the situation—where he finds that it is needed. The fact that the person who models such life in action is a Samaritan, an outsider to Israel on whom the Jews looked with hostility and contempt, gives an added force to Jesus' riposte.

Perhaps there are also links between the parable of the good Samaritan and the episode in Martha's home. Luke connects the episodes through one of his many references to Jesus' journey (v. 38), but it is unclear how much we should make of Luke's decision to place these two encounters together. The point of Jesus' words (vv. 41–42) may be that Mary focuses on the most important part of hospitality, which is paying attention to one's guest, whereas Martha is distracted by some of the things that she feels she needs to do in order to provide hospitality of a particular kind. Some readers have found in this episode an illustration of what it is to love God—to sit at Jesus' feet and listen to his word (v. 39). If so, its position immediately after the parable of the good Samaritan may be significant, for the parable would show what it is to love one's neighbour while Mary's example would illustrate what is involved in loving God. These are the two points that the lawyer raised (v. 27) in response to Jesus' question about what the Law required of those who would inherit eternal life.

4 The Lord's Prayer

Luke 11:1–13

The version presented by Luke of what we have come to call the Lord's Prayer is much shorter than the version that we use today. Partly, that is because we add the words 'For yours is the kingdom, the power and the glory for ever and ever, Amen' at the end, although they are not included in either of the versions found in the New Testament. Partly, it is because the version that we use is closer to the form found in Matthew than in Luke. Luke's version is the shorter of the two. He does not include the requests 'your will be done on earth as it is in heaven' or 'deliver us from evil', both of which are in Matthew. Also, Luke's form of address—

'Father'—is shorter than that of Matthew, who has 'Our Father in heaven'.

One question sometimes asked is which of these versions is more original. That is difficult to answer. Many scholars believe that much of the teaching of Jesus found in both Matthew and Luke but not in Mark goes back to a source that Matthew and Luke each used in addition to Mark. This source is known as Q (from *Quelle*, the German word for 'source'). Many of these scholars also think that Luke's version of the prayer is closer to the Q version than to that of Matthew. Considering questions about the way in which Matthew and Luke used their sources helps us to see how each writer has shaped and presented the material that he includes. This helps to identify the key points that he wished to make about Jesus. Luke has a particular emphasis on Jesus as one who prays, and here (unlike Matthew) he shows how Jesus' example leads his disciples to ask him to teach them to pray (vv. 1–2).

We too may follow the model prayer that Jesus gives (vv. 2–4), either using its words in the form that we know them or taking each of its parts as a stimulus for prayer on similar themes. We too must be persistent in prayer, not because God will answer merely in order to stop us asking, but because he is more responsive and well-disposed to our requests than any friend that we may have (vv. 5–12). Even human parents give good gifts to their children; God will give even more to his children, not least the Holy Spirit to those who ask him (v. 13).

5 Sign of the kingdom

Luke 11:14–26

The division that Jesus brings among the people to whom he has come is seen in their differing responses to this exorcism. Some are amazed (v. 14), but others have a negative response. One group accuses him of colluding with Beelzebul, described here as the ruler of the demons and to be identified with Satan (v. 18; compare 10:17–18). Another tests him (as previously the devil had done, 4:1–3) by demanding a sign from heaven. They cannot see the sign from heaven that Jesus has already performed in their presence.

Jesus' opponents do not question that God can empower exorcists (v. 19), so Jesus' answer to them is concerned to refute their slur against him. The first part makes the point that Beelzebul is unlikely to turn against those who serve him, for he would not wish to destroy his own kingdom (vv. 17–18). In the second, Jesus goes on the offensive. His exorcism is a sign that God's kingdom has come to these people through Jesus, for it is by 'the finger of God' that Jesus casts out demons. 'Finger of God' is a striking phrase which may allude to Exodus 8:19. Just as once God acted through Moses and Aaron to rescue his people from oppression, so now he acts through Jesus. Jesus is stronger than Satan, whose kingdom God is overthrowing (vv. 21–22). Neither Satan's army (the demons) nor his castle and his armour can withstand the finger of God.

Those whom Jesus rescues cannot afford to be smug or complacent. Anyone who is not with Jesus is not neutral but against him (v. 23). Evil may return with even greater effects if those previously released from its bonds fail to respond positively to the one who has delivered them and to transfer their allegiance to him (vv. 24–26). Evil, like nature, abhors a vacuum. Jesus calls those whom he meets to commit themselves to him and to the kingdom of God. We should not delay but should seek to be filled with the Spirit that his Father longs to give (11:13).

6 A call for a response

Luke 11:27–36

A woman praises Jesus by praising the mother who has raised him, but Jesus rebuffs her words: 'Blessed rather are those who hear the word of God and obey it' (v. 28). Jesus returns again to the theme expressed in his parable of the wise and foolish builders (6:46–49) and in his description of all those who hear the word of God and do it, as his mother and his brothers (8:21). The response that Jesus requires is not admiration but practical commitment to his cause, for even those who marvel at his ministry, but do not join him, are against him (11:23).

Jesus' call to commitment is followed by a call to repentance (vv. 29–32) and a number of sayings about light (vv. 33–36). In Matthew's Gospel (12:40), the 'sign of Jonah' refers to Jesus' burial and resurrection. Here in Luke (vv. 29–32), the sign is Jesus, the one who, like Jonah, preached repentance. Jonah's non-Israelite audience in Nineveh heard and repented, and the non-Israelite queen of Sheba came to Solomon to listen to him. Jesus is greater than Solomon, yet the Israelites to whom he preaches are less receptive to his word than were those who heard Jonah and Solomon. Luke issues a warning to all who are complacent about their status before God, that they must make sure to listen and respond to the prophet whom he sends.

Insofar as Jesus' words about the proper positioning of a lamp (v. 33) relate to what has gone before, Jesus appears to be referring to himself as the lamp. He preaches publicly, so that others may hear his words. Not all receive them, however. Some hear and see who he is—those whose eyes are healthy—but others do not (vv. 34–36). These sayings are difficult to understand, but in their present context they seem to point to our need to make careful choices about what we hear and what we see. Choosing not to hear and see the significance of Jesus now may lessen our ability to do so in the future, as it allows the darkness within us to grow. We are reminded that Jesus is a light for revelation to the Gentiles as well as a sign that will be opposed (2:32, 34), and of our need to listen to, and to stand with, him.

Guidelines

When Jesus' disciples ask Jesus to teach them to pray, it seems as if they are responding to the example that Jesus has set them (11:1). Luke frequently depicts Jesus at prayer, often at important points in his narrative. Most recently Luke has depicted Jesus praying joyfully after the return of the 70, when he gave thanks that God had revealed to them what he had not revealed to others (10:21–22). Here Jesus rejoices at what has already happened—perhaps itself an answer to prayer? Elsewhere he teaches of the need for persistence in prayer, and reminds us that God longs to give us the Spirit (11:5–13; compare 18:1–8).

Jesus teaches us to be persistent in prayer, yet each of us probably knows what it is to pray persistently for something and not to see it happen. What are we doing and what do we expect to happen (and to whom) when we pray for the chronically sick but see no change in their condition, or watch them die? What are we doing and what do we expect to happen when we continue to pray for peace in the Middle East or elsewhere, yet see and read news reports of apparently unending violence? Jesus' teaching that we should be persistent in prayer is clear, even if it may be less clear what we are doing when we engage in intercession. What does the shorter form of the Lord's Prayer that Luke records suggest to us about the nature and purpose of the prayers in which we are taught to be persistent?

1 Right and wrong priorities

Luke 11:37–54

This is the second occasion when Jesus enters into controversy with a Pharisee who is host at a meal but fails to treat him with the courtesy due to a guest (see 7:36–50). The Pharisee reveals his indignation when Jesus does not wash in order to make himself ritually pure before the meal (v. 38). Jesus has failed to practise the religious observances that his host considers necessary; next he proceeds to attack his host because he does not consider that such external ritual actions are necessary. What matters more is the inner disposition of people before God their maker (vv. 39–40).

This disposition towards God is reflected by the disposition to others in need to which it leads. By noting how the Pharisees tithe herbs that might be used to season food, but omitting any reference to their tithing the grain that would provide the substance to be seasoned, Jesus attacks the Pharisees for their wrong priorities. They focus on details but fail to attend to justice and the love of God (v. 42). They might follow at least some of the law about tithing, but have lost sight of the purpose for which it was given—that those in need might be provided with enough to live on. These Pharisees, like the lawyers who are with them, have lost sight of the reason behind the rules they now impose on others (v. 46). Rather than helping others, they have obscured for them the purpose of God's law. They have imposed burdens on them but have not shared with them the understanding and discernment that would help them to live more faithfully as God's people in God's land (v. 47). Neither by their teaching nor by their example are they of any use to the people whom they are supposed to be helping (v. 52).

Whether Jesus' strong words of condemnation are directed at Pharisees

29

and lawyers as a whole or at those individuals present with him at this meal is unclear. What is clear, however, is their application to all who might influence others who seek to follow God. Both what we say and what we do are important. We are called not to load burdens on others but to take practical steps to help them carry their load (v. 46). We should not take away the key of knowledge and hinder others from entering where it leads (v. 52), and should be sure that we do not find ourselves opposing those whom God has sent (v. 49). This is easy to say, but often more difficult to do. Even those who begin with the best of intentions may become as these Pharisees and lawyers were.

2 The judgment and love of God

Luke 12:1–12

Jesus' condemnation of the hypocrisy of the Pharisees is now used as a warning to his disciples. The thought that anything we have said or whispered in private will be laid bare to public scrutiny is alarming and reminds us that none of us is without cause for reproach. Were this to happen, we would be subject to the censure of others who would begin to see us as God already does (compare 11:40). Yet any fear that we might have of other people should be as nothing compared to our fear of God. Other people, at worst, could kill us; the authority of God extends even beyond death itself (v. 5). Jesus' words are chilling to those who acknowledge their own sinfulness, even if much of it remains hidden from those around us, but may offer hope to those without adequate resources or any human champion to defend them. In this context they may have particular application to the inner reality of our response to Jesus and how it leads us to behave when others are not watching.

Jesus' presentation of God and his authority is tempered by and intertwined with his presentation of God as the one who knows, sustains and cares for each of us. The one whom we are to fear is one who is just and gracious. How we respond to Jesus, whom he sends, will affect how Jesus responds to us when we come before him for judgment (vv. 8–9). Particularly chilling are Jesus' words of warning that whoever blasphemes against the Holy Spirit will not be forgiven (v. 10). Luke does not make clear what this saying means. In Mark (3:29), it appears to refer to the accusation that Jesus is inspired not by the Spirit of God but by an unclean spirit. Here in Luke, it may perhaps relate to the words that follow: those who blaspheme against the Holy Spirit are those who reject the testimony that the Spirit gives to them when they are on trial (vv. 11–12). If we may turn to Acts for help, there are references there to those who test or oppose the Holy Spirit (Acts 5:32, 7:51). Many other suggestions have also been made, but it does not seem possible to reach a decisive answer about the interpretation of this saying.

As in Jesus' words about God both as judge and as one who has counted even the hairs of our head (vv. 4–6), so here the threat of judgment for blasphemy against the Spirit is intertwined with the promise of his help (vv. 10–12).

3 Possessions and God's provision

Luke 12:13–34

Jesus refuses to be drawn by a family dispute, but takes the question that he is asked as an opportunity to give teaching of his own. In verses 13–21 he addresses the crowd through the person who has spoken to him; in verses 22–34 he turns instead to his disciples, his 'little flock' (v. 32).

In the parable of the rich fool, Luke presents Jesus once again as showing how a person's attitude towards material riches is symbolic of the person's inner disposition towards God and others. So focused is the rich fool on his own future comfort that he gives no thought to the needs of others around him. So wrapped up is he in his own world that he has no one but himself with whom to discuss his apparent good fortune (v. 19). So warped is his understanding of the world that he fails to be rich towards God, its (and his) Creator (v. 21). Thus he is taken by surprise when his life is demanded of him and all that he has acquired is taken from within his control (v. 20).

That we have no ultimate control over possessions is certainly true, but this is less clearly a comfort to those in need than a warning to the rich. Jesus' teaching to his disciples instructs them not to worry, for worry cannot lengthen their life (v. 25), and assures them of God's provision (vv. 22–24). Such words stand in tension with our knowledge that many of God's children do not have the food or shelter that they need today, and challenge us to consider how we may work to alleviate their needs, whether through sharing our own resources, using those resources to effect change ourselves, or lobbying our government and others in positions of influence. Perhaps, too, they challenge us to raise our eyes beyond the horizons of this world. We need not be distracted from struggling for justice for all people today even if we rejoice in the prospect of treasure in heaven. Our treasure there may depend on how we use such wealth as we have already been given in the present (vv. 33–34; see v. 21). Our life does not consist in the abundance of possessions (v. 15), but how we use the abundance that we have affects other lives as well as our own. If we avoid greed, both we and others will benefit.

4 Authority and responsibility

Luke 12:35–48

Jesus continues to make connections between the way in which we lead our lives today and the extent to which we are prepared for his return at an unexpected hour. This warning that we need to be ready follows naturally from his teaching about the need to store up treasure not on earth but in heaven. An awareness of a heavenly reality that we are yet to enjoy may provide some motivation for what we do in the meantime, but the focus of these parables is clearly on the here and now. Christians are not called to have their heads in the clouds but to be engaged in practical discipleship here on earth. Watchfulness and alertness are important, but they find their focus in the faithful discharge of daily duties (vv. 35–40).

Peter's question (v. 41) is the literary vehicle that allows Luke to introduce more of Jesus' teaching on a similar topic. The question also provides a more specific focus for Jesus' teaching, for now Jesus shows that those whom he has called (the 'us' of verse 41, which refers to the disciples on whose behalf Peter speaks) must be particularly mindful of their responsibility to be ready for his return. They are to be faithful both to the master whom they serve and to others over whom they have authority and for whom they are also responsible. They must live up to the responsibility and authority with which they are entrusted, and will be judged accordingly (vv. 42–48).

Jesus' words remind us of the responsibilities that come with positions of leadership in the Church, but once again Jesus' warnings of judgment are tempered by a reminder of the goodness of the one who is our judge. Jesus' picture of the returning master eating with and serving his slaves (v. 37) overturns both ancient and contemporary notions of hierarchy and the status quo. Jesus who knocks at the door comes in and eats with us and invites us to eat with him (Revelation 3:20).

5 Division and discernment

Luke 12:49–59

Jesus' teaching on judgment continues with a reminder that he is a cause of division (vv. 51–53; compare 2:34–35) and that each of us must decide on our own response to him. We are presented with a strong warning to turn to Jesus and repent, or perish. Characteristically for Luke's Gospel, the indication of whether or not we have responded accordingly will be the way in which we use our possessions (v. 58).

Jesus' words 'I have a baptism with which to be baptized' (v. 50) most probably refer to his coming passion. It is as much a part of God's plan that he must complete as is the division that he will bring. Jesus' words about dividing families are shocking and warn against any complacent appeal to 'family values' as the core of Christian discipleship.

The final sayings that Luke presents here may offer two perspectives on the need for discernment. In verses 54–56, he criticizes the crowds who can interpret the weather from a distance but cannot interpret what is going on in their midst as God's prophet speaks to them. Although meteorologically sensitive, they are religiously insensitive and therefore blind to what God, through Jesus, is doing in their midst.

The link between verses 57–59 and what has gone before is by no means clear. Perhaps it suggests the need to show practical wisdom—prudence, perhaps, or even common sense—in difficult situations in daily life. Perhaps it is another warning for Jesus' hearers to prepare to repent and follow him rather than face him as their judge.

Almost certainly significant is the presence of the words 'on the way' (v. 58). Even now, as Jesus travels to Jerusalem, he addresses those who are 'on the way' with him. Jesus may bring division, but he advises those who can be reconciled to others to make an effort to settle their differences (v. 58). The consequences of failure to do so will be great (v. 59).

6 Repentance and religiosity

Luke 13:1–21

Both the news that Pilate has killed some Galileans and Jesus' reference to the death of Jerusalemites killed by the collapse of a tower give Jesus an opportunity to call his audience to repentance. It is not that there is any connection between the lives of those who have died and the fates that they met. His point is rather that death comes unexpectedly, so those given the chance to repent must take it while there is time (vv. 3, 5). This seems also to be the point of the parable of the fig tree (vv. 6–9). There (it is implied), the owner of the tree grants a stay of execution to the gardener who asks for yet more time for the tree to bear fruit. His request (we assume) is allowed, but the time that he asks for is firmly limited, not indefinite (v. 9).

Less clear is the relationship between this teaching on repentance and the miracle (vv. 10–17) and the two parables (vv. 18–21) that follow. The healing of this crippled woman, recorded only by Luke, recalls earlier controversies in which Jesus declared himself Lord of the sabbath (6:5). Once again Jesus' religious opponents accuse him of failing to honour God's law and once again Jesus puts compassion and the relief of suffering before such religious scruples. Jesus' suggestion that his opponents seem to care more for animals than for people (v. 15) takes on quite unexpected associations in our contemporary world where some people will threaten to kill other humans in order to prevent the use of animals in medical research.

Jesus is not only Lord over the sabbath but also the one before whom Satan flees (v. 16). However we understand the nature of the link between Satan's rule and human illness, Jesus is stronger than any opponent. Just as the kingdom of God may grow from a small seed (vv. 18–19), so in healings such as this the kingdom advances as Jesus continues towards Jerusalem. Jesus' opponents are put to shame, but the crowds see and rejoice (v. 17). Once again we are challenged as to whose example we will follow. Jesus' presence provokes division and neutrality is not an option (compare 11:23).

Guidelines

Luke pays careful attention to identifying the various audiences that Jesus addresses at different points. Thus, in our last six readings, we have seen Jesus address the Pharisees and lawyers and other religious leaders (11:39, 46; 13:15), the crowds (12:15, 54) and the disciples (12:1, 22). Probably most of us will identify most naturally with the disciples. Probably we should. But is there a danger that if we assume we are those who are right with God—those who follow Jesus as we should—we might end up more like the Pharisees? Might we end up ceasing to hear and do God's word because we are so sure of our own interpretation of his word that we lose sight of what it is really about? Might we end up placing limits on God's love and compassion and therefore excluding the contemporary equivalents of those people on the margins of society to whom Jesus came and with whom he sat and ate? Although we look respectable and devout to ourselves and to those like us, might we end up becoming an obstacle between others and the love that God has for them?

1 God's purpose and goal

Luke 13:22–35

Luke's reference to Jesus passing 'through one town and village after another, teaching as he made his way to Jerusalem' marks the beginning of the second half of the travel narrative. We have here characteristic teaching of the prophet on his journey (vv. 24–30) and also further teaching on the necessity of the fate that Jesus must meet in Jerusalem (vv. 32–35). Luke's reference to Herod may be significant. Shortly before, he has mentioned Pilate as the one who killed Galileans who had come to the temple (13:1), an ominous note in an account of other Galileans who are also travelling to Jerusalem. Now Luke reminds us of the foreboding presence of Herod in the background of his narrative. Together with Pilate, he will seal Jesus' fate (23:6–12).

It is not, of course, that either Herod or Pilate is in control. Perhaps Herod may already wish to kill Jesus, but since this news is brought by

Pharisees (v. 31; compare 9:9 for Luke's own explanation as to Herod's intentions towards Jesus), whom Luke portrays as Jesus' opponents, we do not know if it is a genuine warning or intended as a trap. Yet God remains in control and Jesus remains obedient to him. Jesus goes to Jerusalem not to flee Herod (who ruled in Galilee) but in conformity to the purpose of God—'because it is impossible for a prophet to be killed away from Jerusalem' (v. 33).

For readers familiar with the story of Jesus, this reference to his finishing his work on the third day (v. 32) cannot but evoke thoughts of the resurrection. For readers attuned to Luke's particular understanding of that event, it will also evoke the ascension. At the end of his Gospel, Luke presents the ascension as happening on the same day as Jesus' resurrection and bringing it to its completion. Already, at the beginning of the travel narrative, he has also made clear that the ascension is the goal of Jesus' journey (9:51). Jesus is but half way along his journey, but Luke reminds us again why Jesus is on the road and what will happen to him in Jerusalem. Jesus feels love and compassion for the city and its people (v. 34), yet they will reject him just as they have rejected other prophets whom God has sent. Therefore they will suffer as a result (v. 35).

2 Reversal of fortunes

Luke 14:1–14

Luke inserts his third account of Jesus healing on the sabbath and the controversy that ensues into an account of Jesus sharing a meal in the house of a Pharisee. The Pharisees are watching him closely (v. 1), which suggests their hostility, and Jesus both acts and speaks in ways that demonstrate an authority that cuts across both religious conventions and the sort of behaviour that a host might expect of his guest. In the house of another Pharisee, Jesus has criticized his host for not acting hospitably towards his guest (7:36–50); here Jesus criticizes both his fellow guests (vv. 7–11) and, at least implicitly, his host (vv. 12–14).

The point that Jesus makes to his fellow guests is summed up in verse 11. He is not giving tips on etiquette to explain the appropriate way in which to be honoured or exalted at the table, but questioning the appropriateness of the desire to be honoured at all. Real honour comes not from seeking it but being given it by others, the most important of whom is God. What really counts is whether we are exalted or humbled by God, who can and will reverse merely human attempts at self-exaltation as well as human humility. The sort of reversal that Jesus speaks of here echoes the reversal proclaimed by his mother before his birth (1:51–55). This is a theme to which Luke will have Jesus return: verse 11 is repeated almost word-for-word at 18:14.

Jesus' words to his host (vv. 12–14) concern not self-ambition or status-seeking but the need to give to others without any expectation of receiving from them in return. Perhaps these words are a rebuke to the host for inviting Jesus to a meal not in order to share with him but to find an opportunity to catch him out (v. 1). Certainly they pick up Luke's interest in the reversal of fortunes that Jesus brings, and his challenge to traditional understandings of reciprocity as the basis for social relationships. We are not to give invitations to others of equal social standing, because that will oblige them to give invitations to us in return. Rather, we are to give on the basis of need, without thought of recompense or reward. Such is God's love towards us. Any reward there may be will come when we are included among the righteous at the resurrection (v. 14).

3 The cost of discipleship

Luke 14:15–35

Jesus' parable about the guests invited to a great dinner (vv. 15–24) speaks both of the generosity of God and the need of those invited to respond appropriately to their invitations. Thus this parable, addressed to those with whom Jesus was himself at a meal, leads into and prepares the way for the teaching on the cost of discipleship that Jesus offers to the crowds (vv. 25–35).

Each person who is told that the banquet is now ready (v. 17) has already received and accepted an invitation. Thus, the refusal to attend involves going back on commitments that they have already made. In each case, the reason is the same: something else has cropped up since they accepted their invitation, so each person looks to his own interests rather than to the need to respect the person whose invitation he had accepted but now spurns. Each is concerned with his own material affairs to such an extent that he cannot see beyond them. Given the context in which the parable is told, it is hard not to identify those who are insulting the host as the religiously respectable Jewish leaders, such as the Pharisees and lawyers with whom Jesus is at dinner. God had invited them to his banquet but they have become too preoccupied with their own concerns to receive the benefits of his invitation. God therefore turns to those on the margins of Jewish society—the poor, crippled, lame and blind in the streets and lanes of the town (v. 21)—as well as those outside its boundaries (v. 23). Thus, Luke has Jesus foreshadowing the inclusion of the Gentiles within the people of God.

Jesus' words to the crowd make explicit the need to count the cost in following him. There is no point in accepting an invitation but then becoming too distracted to reap its rewards. His words about hating one's family (v. 26) point to the need for passionate commitment, exemplified by a readiness to put nothing at all before God and his call. His words about building a tower, laying a foundation and planning for war (vv. 28–32) speak also of the need for sober reflection and an awareness of what long-term commitment will cost. Following Jesus means not only carrying the cross and following him (v. 27) but also sitting lightly to our possessions (v. 33). This is what the first guests invited to the dinner found themselves unable to do.

4 Seeking and welcoming the lost

Luke 15:1–32

Although we often read it on its own, Luke presents the parable of the lost (or prodigal) son as one of three: lost sheep (vv. 3–7), lost coin (vv. 8–10), lost son (vv. 11–32). Reading them together helps to show that each makes a similar point. A sinner is lost, then found, and there is great joy in heaven as a result. Jesus' opponents find cause for reproach in his custom of welcoming sinners and eating with them (v. 2). Jesus responds by claiming that this is precisely what God longs to do—and is doing now, through him. The repentance of a sinner is cause not for complaint but for rejoicing (vv. 7, 10, 32). So great is God's desire to restore to relationship with him even one person who is lost that he is like a shepherd who will leave the rest of the flock in the wilderness (a high-risk strategy) and go after the one that is lost *until he finds it* (v. 4). Luke emphasizes the persistence of God in seeking the lost sheep.

One difficulty in reading parables is deciding whether they are stories that make one or two points, or allegories in which different characters and episodes stand for people and events outside the parable. If there is an element of allegory in the parable of the lost son, then those who grumble about the radical inclusiveness of Jesus' ministry may be reflected in his depiction of the older son who becomes angry and sulks (v. 28) rather than rejoicing at his brother's return. The older son's exaggeration of his brother's sin (v. 30; compare v. 13) betrays both a lack of grace and also undue confidence in his own goodness. Perhaps, too, it recalls the Pharisees and scribes who identify others as sinners with whom they will not mix (vv. 1–2). If so, the parable shows how their behaviour is as worthy of reproach as that of the elder son. Just as the younger son distanced himself from his father by leaving home, so the older son distances himself by refusing to share in the celebration and questioning the father's generosity (vv. 29–30), yet the father loves them both.

Whether or not such an allegorical reading is justified, the attitude of the elder son stands as a warning to us of how ugly we become if we fail to rejoice when God brings sinners (people that we think are not like us?) into the same celebratory meal to which we too are invited as God's guests. Courtesy to our host demands that we are courteous to all his guests.

5 A puzzling parable

Luke 16:1–13

Time and time again, Luke presents Jesus as teaching about the need to use material possessions appropriately, for the way in which we use them reveals much of our inner disposition towards God and towards others. This parable is one of many passages in Luke that reflect this theme and are found only in his Gospel, but it is by no means clear what it means. Even the point at which the parable finishes is uncertain. Most probably, it is after verse 8a ('and his master commended the dishonest manger because he had acted shrewdly'), which would mean that it is followed by three applications: verses 8b–9, verses 10–12 and verse 13. If this is the case, Luke may be bringing together sayings that were independent of each other before he presented them in this way. Perhaps the way in which he does so suggests that questions about how the parable is to be understood arose at a very early stage in the process by which it came to Luke.

Surely Jesus does not commend dishonesty, especially when it is at someone else's expense? Yet that is what the parable seems to imply. The manager is about to lose his job because he has been squandering his master's assets, and responds by cooking the books. He reduces the debts that others owe to his master (vv. 5–7) in order that these people might show him kindness. Presumably this will be at the master's expense, not at his own, but we are not told enough to be certain. Yet the master who is sacking him for previously squandering his assets now commends him for his shrewdness! Perhaps the key to the parable lies in emphasizing not the sharp practice of the manager but his shrewdness. On this reading, disciples are not encouraged to be dishonest but are warned of the need to be prudent.

Were they not preceded by this parable, Jesus words in verses 10–13 would be straightforward to understand, but that does not make them any easier to obey.

6 The rich man and Lazarus

Luke 16:14–31

Luke continues to emphasize Jesus' teaching on the importance of the way in which we use our money, by describing the Pharisees as lovers of money (v. 14). In this context it is tantamount to saying that their love of money makes them enemies towards God, whose prophet they ridicule for his teaching. Jesus criticizes them and then pronounces on the subject of the law in general and its lasting force, and on the particular case of divorce. Why Luke places these sayings here is unclear: there is no obvious reason to connect them with either what precedes or what follows them.

The parable of the rich man and Lazarus returns to the theme of the importance of using possessions properly, and connects it with teaching about judgment and God's inversion of human social arrangements. The parable is found only in Luke and is the only parable in which a protagonist, Lazarus, is given a name. The rich man is morally culpable for the lack of care that he has shown to his neighbour in need, although Lazarus shows no virtue simply by being poor. Yet by contrasting Lazarus' condition as a poor man (v. 20) with that of the rich man (v. 19) outside whose gate he lay, Luke reminds us of the first of Jesus' beatitudes and woes (6:20, 24). The parable enacts the radical reversal of which Jesus spoke, as anticipated in the words of Mary on the news of his conception (1:50–55). Lazarus is a rich fool who was not rich to God or to others, so now he will pay the price (compare 12:15–21). He is not in Hades simply for being rich but for not sharing his resources with others, yet still he thinks that he may call on Lazarus to serve him (vv. 24, 27).

Abraham's words about the rich man's brothers refusing to repent even if someone rises from the dead have unmistakable resonance for those who read this story in the light of faith in the resurrected and ascended Jesus. Not even Jesus' resurrection convinced many of his contemporaries to believe in him; little wonder that they failed to grasp and to live in accordance with what they read in the books of Moses and the prophets (vv. 30–31).

Luke's depiction of Lazarus and the poor man as each being conscious of their position after death may be compared to Jesus' promise to the thief that today he would be with him in Paradise (23:43). Luke's perspective on what happens after we die emphasizes the immediate experience of the individual, but the parable is more concerned with how we must live today than with what will become of us after death.

Guidelines

Meals and tables are of great symbolic importance in the ministry of Jesus, particularly as Luke presents it. Lazarus is excluded from the rich man's table but is welcomed to Abraham's side. Jesus himself dines frequently and uses the occasion presented in chapter 14 both to criticize those who use meals as an opportunity to elevate themselves at the expense of others and also to evoke the nature of heaven. The master in his parable brings to his banquet (14:21) those whom we are told to invite to our meals (v. 13). The way we share hospitality with others should mirror the way that God is gracious and inviting to us and to all on the margins. Is this true of the way in which we live our lives in the churches and other communities of which each of us is a part?

1 Faith and gratitude

Luke 17:1–19

Jesus continues to teach his disciples on four topics, not obviously related to each other: the danger of stumbling blocks (vv. 1–3a), the necessity of forgiveness (vv. 3b–4), a saying on the power of Christian faith (vv. 5–6) and another on the inadequacy of Christian service (vv. 7–10). If anything binds them together, perhaps each bears in some way on the demands of discipleship.

Jesus' words about not causing others to stumble and being always ready to forgive whenever someone repents seem straightforward enough to understand, but are less easy to implement in our daily lives. His reply to his disciples' request that he increase their faith suggests that what little faith they have is not even the size of a mustard seed (v. 6). We may recall the lack of faith that they have shown before (9:43), but we must note that they seek for more, and strive to follow their example. Yet, even if we do, we must remember that we are to expect no reward simply for behaving as disciples should—for not causing others to stumble, for forgiving those who repent and for serving our master as he expects. That seems to be the force of Jesus' parable about the slave and his master (vv. 7–10). It is hardly a comfort.

The fact that we are to thank and praise God, even if we should not expect thanks from him for merely doing what we are commanded, is apparent from the healing story that follows. Luke reminds us that Jesus is on his way to Jerusalem and refers also to Samaria (v. 11), probably to introduce a story in which the only person to praise God and thank Jesus for his healing is a Samaritan (v. 16). In this story, unique to his Gospel, Luke shows how, in Jesus, God reaches out both to members of his chosen people and to another on whom Israelites looked with scorn. The failure of all but the despised outsider reminds us of our need not to be complacent about our status before God, and not to look down on others whose responses may prove more appropriate than our own. We may be no more than worthless slaves (v. 10), but we ought always to thank God for what he has done for us and be ready for him to do the same for others, too.

2 Kingdom and end-time

Luke 17:20–37

The Pharisees' question about when the kingdom of God would come reminds Luke's readers that they cannot see what is happening before their eyes. Jesus has spoken often of the kingdom as present or coming, yet it has passed his opponents by. This seems to be the force of Jesus' saying to the Pharisees that the kingdom is 'among you' (so NRSV) or perhaps 'within your reach' (v. 21): it is coming about through what Jesus says and does, yet they cannot see it even when he addresses them.

Jesus then turns to his disciples. His teaching to them demonstrates that the kingdom that has already come is not the same as the end-time, when the Son of Man will be revealed as judge of the living and the dead (see Acts 17:31) and the rule of God will be decisively established for all to see. That time is yet to come. Jesus words here refer briefly to the suffering that he is about to face (v. 25) but most of this material concerns a time further in the future. Those who read the Gospel know that what Jesus is referring to in verse 25 has already happened and is in their past; the rest of what he refers to is yet to come. Luke has Jesus emphasize not the imminence of the days of the Son of Man but their certainty. Those who point to signs of his arrival (v. 23) are to be ignored, but his coming is not in doubt, even if many people do not recognize its importance. Those who saw Noah build the ark did not prepare for the flood but carried on as before, and were therefore destroyed (v. 27). Those who were with Lot in Sodom did not leave but carried on as before, and were therefore also destroyed (v. 29).

Just as certain and as absolute as the fact of the coming of the Son of Man is the division that he will cause. Some of this division has been seen already in Jesus' ministry, just as Simeon had foretold (2:34–35), but more division is yet to come. The way in which one will be taken and another will be left (vv. 34–35) suggests that we may be surprised by the outcome. It reminds us of the absolute sovereignty of God.

3 Parables on prayer

Luke 18:1–14

Jesus now gives his disciples a second parable about the coming of the Son of Man (v. 8). Like the preceding parable (17:20–37), it majors on how

Christians are to live now in the light of what is yet to come. Jesus' emphasis is on the need for persistence in prayer and may be compared to the parable of a friend in need at midnight and the teaching that follows it (11:5–13). As in that earlier parable, God's willingness to answer those who pray to him (v. 7) is contrasted with the unwillingness of the judge who grants the widow justice only to get peace for himself (vv. 3–4). There is no question that God will hear our prayer; the question is rather whether we will persist in prayer (vv. 7–8).

Jesus' second parable on prayer changes the focus from the need for persistence in prayer to the need to pray in an appropriate spirit. Jesus addresses this parable not to his disciples but 'to some who trusted in themselves that they were righteous and regarded others with contempt' (v. 9). His words serve as a warning to those who are too confident about their own status before God, as well as being another illustration of God's desire to show mercy to sinners who repent (compare 15:7, 10, 32). We need to be careful not to assume too easily that we are like the tax collector, in case we end up like the Pharisee as a result. The conclusion to the parable (v. 14) is almost identical to the conclusion of Jesus' teaching about not taking seats of honour at a wedding banquet (14:11). We need to be humble before God as well as before other people.

The fact that Jesus sets this parable in the temple is a reminder of the destination of his journey.

4 The dangers of wealth

Luke 18:15–30

Most of us see independence as a virtue, even if, at the same time, we often underestimate the extent to which we rely on God and on others in all that we do. One way to understand Jesus' two encounters that we read about today, one with little children (vv. 15–17) and the other with a ruler (vv. 18–25), is to note the contrast between the level of dependence that is available to young children (literally 'babies' or 'infants': Mark and Matthew have Jesus speaking of little children, but Luke does not) and that which the ruler who puts his question to Jesus could expect to enjoy. Infants cannot but depend on others for everything that they need, but those who are rich and influential can use their money and contacts to try to insulate themselves against whatever life may throw at them. Jesus' words that the kingdom of God belongs to those such as infants (v. 16) reminds us of our need to rely wholeheartedly, unselfconsciously and entirely on God, not on material possessions. His words to the rich young ruler warn us what may happen if we put our trust in our material resources and let them come between us and following Jesus (vv. 22–24).

Jesus' paradoxical words about the camel and the eye of the needle ought to be taken literally, not rationalized away by reference to some sort of putative gate through which a camel may squeeze if only it tries very hard. These words are frighteningly close to saying that it is impossible for the rich to enter the kingdom of God. The astonished reaction of the disciples (v. 26) and Jesus' reply (v. 27) show that his first disciples were no less shocked than we are if we let the force of these words sink in. All that we possess might come between us and God if we hold on to it when we should not, just as it did for this morally upright and religiously faithful man (v. 21). Jesus' words to him about the dangers of wealth appear to be spoken less in anger than in sorrow (vv. 22–24). This warning that he gives to all who put their wealth before his call on their lives is contrasted to his words to Peter that all who put first the kingdom of God will be amply rewarded both in this age and in the age to come (vv. 29–30).

5 Two encounters with Jesus

Luke 18:31—19:10

Jesus' third foretelling of his death and resurrection (18:31–34) reminds Luke's readers of the reason for Jesus' journey. Two references to Jericho (18:35; 19:1) also help to maintain a sense of movement as Jesus draws closer to the city in which prophets meet their fate. Luke has already told us that Jericho is not far from Jerusalem (10:30). Bartimaeus and Zacchaeus each make an effort to encounter Jesus despite physical limitations (18:35–39; 19:2–4) and both respond to Jesus in a fitting manner when he engages with them (18:41–43; 19:5–10).

Bartimaeus and Zacchaeus are saved through their encounters with Jesus (18:42; 19:10). Thus each of them is an answer to the question 'Then who can be saved?' raised by the disciples back in 18:26. Bartimaeus is a beggar but Zacchaeus is wealthy, so perhaps rich people can be saved, provided that—like Zacchaeus—they are prepared to share a significant amount of their wealth with others.

One question that we might ask about Zacchaeus is whether his expression of generosity to the poor and his concern to compensate those whom he may have defrauded is something that he promises to do in the future as a consequence of meeting Jesus, or is a practice that he already follows. Because the NRSV translates his words in verse 8 as 'I will give' and 'I will pay back', it suggests that he is referring to something he is about to do for the first time. But the verb behind these words might also be translated 'I give' and 'I pay back'. That would imply that Zacchaeus was already generous and honest, even before he met Jesus. He did not knowingly extort from others, as John had warned that tax collectors should not, but generously compensated those whom he may have cheated. He also already gave regularly to the poor, thus indicating a proper disposition to God, yet did so while remaining rich. Whichever interpretation we prefer, the example of Zacchaeus offers hope that perhaps some who are wealthy may nevertheless enter the kingdom of God. Although treated by many as an outcast because of his profession, Zacchaeus too is a son of Abraham (v. 9).

6 Kingdom present or future?

Luke 19:11–27

Luke has Jesus tell this story as, at last, he draws near to Jerusalem (v. 11). Thus it holds a climactic place in his travel narrative. Luke also tells us that Jesus told this parable not only because he was near Jerusalem but also because his disciples supposed that the kingdom of God was to appear immediately. He does not state explicitly whether the parable is to refute that notion and explain that there will be a delay before the kingdom comes, or to endorse their belief and explain to them more of what it means for the kingdom of God to appear. Our answer to that question depends on how we understand the parable.

If we are to read it in the light of what Jesus has already taught, we might do well to remember the distinction he has made between the end-time that is yet to come and the kingdom of God that is already a present reality in and through his ministry (see 17:20–25). Jesus' earlier teachings on the presence of the kingdom and on Jerusalem as the place to which his ministry is leading both suggest that the parable is more probably told to help the disciples understand better what the kingdom of God will entail than to counter their belief in its imminence.

Against this, the fact that the nobleman sets off to a distant country on a journey that gives at least some of his slaves time to profit from the money that he has left them may suggest that some time passes before he returns with royal power. On this reading, perhaps the parable is intended to offset the disciples' belief that the kingdom of God is about to appear immediately. If so, that would mean that, here, 'kingdom of God' refers to the end-time and that Jesus is speaking of his second coming rather than his entry to Jerusalem at the end of his journey. It is difficult to be sure, although I tend to see the parable as commenting on Jesus' imminent arrival in Jerusalem, not his return on the day of judgment.

On either reading, the nobleman is Jesus and he is given the royal power that is his own. Those who use faithfully the resources with which they are entrusted are rewarded (vv. 15–19), those who do nothing with them are stripped of what they have (vv. 20–24) and those who oppose his reign are slaughtered (v. 27). This is a shocking image, but underlines the consequences of our decision as to whether or not we acknowledge Jesus' rightful rule over our lives. This is the question with which we are left as the king is about to enter the city to which he has been travelling.

Guidelines

Time and time again, Luke emphasizes the importance of the way we use our money and material resources, because it points towards our true disposition towards others and towards God. But the range of results to which this may lead is bewildering. Jesus' words to the rich ruler should fill us with alarm, yet his words to Zacchaeus fill us with hope. Zacchaeus continued to have riches, yet was generous in sharing them with others. We are all warned not to become selfish like the rich fool, who focused on himself without reference to others (12:16–21), or like the rich man who left Lazarus at his gate (16:19–21). But perhaps few of us are called to give up everything, like the young ruler was (18:22). Certainly most of us would find it easier to think that we were allowed to retain at least some of our resources, provided that we used them in the service of Jesus and of others (8:3; 16:10–13; 19:11–26).

Much as we might like to be given rules about what all this might mean, Luke does not have Jesus give them. If he did, perhaps we would all stick to the minimum of ten per cent or whatever else we thought God might demand. More challenging, but more fitting for those who would live not by the letter but by the spirit of the law, is the example of Zacchaeus. The Mosaic Law gave different stipulations about what should be paid as restitution to those whom individuals had cheated. Zacchaeus' policy of paying back four times anything that he might wrongfully take shows that he chose not the lightest but the most demanding of these stipulations, and his decision to give half his possessions to the poor far exceeds the legal requirements of tithing. Jesus gives no targets that all of us must meet, but calls us to be generous. He leaves it to us to decide the figures in which such generosity might result.

FURTHER READING

Commentaries on the Gospel according to Luke:

Luke Timothy Johnson, *The Gospel of Luke*, The Liturgical Press, 1991.

Judith Lieu, *The Gospel of Luke* (Epworth Commentaries), Epworth Press, 1997.

Henry Wansbrough, *Luke* (The People's Bible Commentary), BRF, 1998.

Studies of Luke's thought:

Stephen Barton, *The Spirituality of the Gospels*, SPCK, 1992, ch. 3.

Paul Borgman, *The Way according to Luke: Hearing the Whole Story of Luke-Acts*, Eerdmans, 2006.

Joel Green, *The Theology of the Gospel of Luke*, Cambridge University Press, 1995.

Luke Timothy Johnson, *Sharing Possessions: Mandate and Symbol of Faith*, SCM, 1981 (out of print).

Christopher Tuckett, *Luke* (T&T Clark Study Guides), Continuum, 2004.

RUTH

In these notes, I wish to focus on the character of Ruth herself rather than dealing with the book as a whole, and this criterion will decide the choice of passages (using the NRSV translation). Perhaps the most surprising thing about the book of Ruth is that it exists as a separate book in the Old Testament canon. Apart from Esther, no other biblical woman has the honour of a book to her name and it is surprising that her story did not become part of a wider narrative, say in the Deuteronomistic history.

The book of Ruth is often seen as a 'family' saga, taking place in Bethlehem in a rural setting. It is not about the politics of the powerful, yet, surprisingly, it reveals links with one of the most famous characters in Israel's history in the genealogy at the end. There is a debate about the dating of the book: is it an early tale about the period of the Judges, perhaps from the early monarchic court, or does the interest in Moabites and the theme of marriage with foreigners place it in post-exilic times? The debates continue among scholars, but in my view the story may well have pre-exilic roots, being retold in fresh contexts later on. The final form of the written text may show some indications of being a later piece of literature. It is a short and vibrant narrative, telling the story with few frills. We have no knowledge of the authorship: it has even been suggested that it was written by a woman, but maybe, given the culture of the time, that is simply wishful thinking.

Ruth as a character has been variously interpreted by feminist scholarship. We might think that she was a 'gift' character to those of this perspective, but her submissiveness both in relation to Naomi, her mother-in-law, and to Boaz, her prospective husband, has made some wonder whether she is such a good role model for feminists after all. This is perhaps slightly unfair, however. Although she sometimes seems to be a pawn in a wider game, she does show initiative of her own. In fact, her decision to stay with her mother-in-law and to adopt a new faith is a bold step in itself.

1 Ruth and Naomi

Ruth 1:6–18

This passage begins at the point where Naomi, widow of Elimelech, who had migrated years before to Moab, decides to return home to Bethlehem in Judah with her two daughters-in-law. Their original reason for migrating was a famine in the home country, but this reason no longer stands. Her two sons have also died in Moab, leaving two Moabite widows. Naomi's suggestion that both Moabite women return to their own homes implies that they are young enough to remarry and live fulfilling lives reunited with their own families.

With Naomi's wish that the Lord (Yahweh, her God) deal kindly with these women, we are introduced to the concept of 'kind dealing' or good deeds that is a theme running through the book. Even non-Israelites can receive God's blessing on the basis of good deeds—a kind of universalism on the basis of good behaviour. Both daughters-in-law are said to have 'dealt kindly' with 'the dead and with me' (v. 8). Amid protestations and weeping, Naomi is firm about their leaving. She then reveals her bitterness at her losses (v. 13), for she feels that her God has turned against her. In verse 20 she says, 'Call me no longer Naomi, call me Mara, for the Almighty has dealt bitterly with me.' Mara means 'bitter', and the suggestion of a name change shows that this emotion runs deep with her. In verse 21, she speaks of her former fullness being turned to emptiness at the hand of God (an experience that will be reversed later in the book). Ruth insists on staying, taking Naomi's people as her people and Naomi's God as her God. It is probably not from religious zeal for Yahweh that Ruth wishes to change her religion, but more from loyalty to her mother-in-law. She shows immense devotion here.

This is our first introduction to Ruth the Moabitess, and two characteristics have already come to the fore—her good deeds for her dead husband and for Naomi, and her unflinching loyalty to Naomi, to the point of calling on the name of Yahweh to witness her loyalty, even in the face of death (v. 17).

2 Ruth meets Boaz

Ruth 2:1–13

In this chapter we are introduced to Naomi's kinsman Boaz, described as 'a prominent rich man'—in today's language, 'a good catch'! Here we see Ruth taking the initiative again as she suggests going out to glean grain, so that she might gain favour by her deeds with 'someone'. She finds herself in Boaz's field (by accident or design?) The next thing we learn of Boaz is that he is a pious man: he blesses his reapers and they respond, in what might be a traditional salutation. Boaz naturally wonders who Ruth is and she is immediately described as a 'Moabitess'. Ruth is for ever labelled as a foreigner among them, even though she has adopted their faith. She is introduced to Boaz by a reaper, who describes her initiative in asking to gather up the grain behind the reapers, her hard work and her commitment.

Boaz then addresses Ruth directly and instructs her to glean only in his field and to refresh herself with the water that his young men have drawn. She is overwhelmed by his generosity and falls prostrate to the ground, thus acknowledging his superior status. Her social position as a widow would be low anyway, but as a foreigner it is lower still. She dares to ask him why she has found favour with him and he reveals that he knows about her good deeds on behalf of Naomi, as well as the detail of her decision to leave Moab. We might wonder if it is Naomi who has filled him in, or others in the Bethlehem community, which can't have been a very big town at the time.

Boaz uses the language of reward for deeds, echoing the words of Naomi at the beginning. Once again the message is that even foreigners who do good deeds can receive God's blessing and his reward. God is described as one who rewards good behaviour (compare the Wisdom literature, notably the prologue and epilogue of the book of Job), as well as one who protects his own. Boaz wishes God's reward and protection upon Ruth. She replies gratefully and reveals how his words have comforted her. They are off to a flying start!

51

3 Boaz's favour

The encounter continues at mealtime when Boaz invites Ruth to eat with him and she takes her fill. Presumably both she and Naomi are hard up at this stage and one wonders how they can afford to put food on the table. As Boaz shows his protection towards Ruth, instructing his young men to let her glean where she likes and even from their own bundles, we get the impression that this is a rather rough workforce—possibly casual labour brought in at harvest time.

Ruth gleans an ephah of barley, which is clearly a good amount, as Naomi is impressed. She shows generosity to Naomi by giving her barley to eat also. When Naomi hears about Boaz, she sees his kindness as a sign from God. It is a return of the Lord's kindness, which had previously departed from her life. Naomi sees this as a turning point in their fortunes, God's kindness extending to the living and the dead (v. 20). Perhaps this is a reference to Boaz being Elimelech's relative: the dead man is therefore not forgotten. We are not told that Boaz shows favour to Ruth because of this kinsmanship, however: the inference is that it is not on such grounds, but merely on the strength of Ruth's good deeds. It is Naomi who now sees an opportunity presenting itself as she reveals Boaz's relationship to them as near kin. When Ruth expresses surprise at Boaz's kindness to her, Naomi's response is to echo Boaz's advice to stay in his field with the other women who are gleaning for the duration of the barley and wheat harvests. It seems that both men and women are in Boaz's employ at this time, the women having the background role of collecting up sheaves that the men have cut.

We are being led through the plot by means of dialogue both in this section and the previous one. Although it is in a primarily narrative setting, this use of dialogue is sophisticated, and leads to the sense of anticipation contained in the story. It is interesting that the theme of kindness continues in this section, with Boaz's kindness to Ruth, on which she particularly remarks to Naomi, and God's kindness as proclaimed by Naomi. It is as if human actions and divine blessing are echoing one another.

4 Ruth at the threshing floor

We join Ruth just about to obey her mother-in-law's instruction as expounded in verses 1–5. Here, Ruth is guided by Naomi and does not take her own initiative, justifying in some way the accusation sometimes made that she is a pawn in a wider game. Boaz is startled when he wakes at midnight to find Ruth, in her best clothes, lying at his uncovered (and hence vulnerable) feet! When he questions who she is, she reveals her kinship relationship to him. The meaning of 'spread your cloak' has been much discussed: could it have sexual innuendoes, even possibly referring to the act of sexual intercourse itself, or is it simply about protection? There does seem to be an element of Ruth giving herself willingly to him, unasked.

Boaz's response of blessing is quite surprising: she can put no foot wrong with him. He interprets her action as an outstanding example of her loyalty. It has to be remembered that he is an older man, probably more of Naomi's generation than Ruth's. When he notes that she has not gone after young men, it seems to be a recognition that in laying herself open to him, she has chosen him, her kinsman, over potentially more attractive possibilities. He calms her fears and reasserts her worth, which could be said to be 'on the line' as a result of this incident. Later in the passage, on his instruction, she slips away before anyone can recognize her (v. 14).

Boaz reveals that there is a nearer kinsman than him who should have first call on Ruth, so he is duty bound to approach the other man before offering to act as next-of-kin for Ruth. He expresses no preference for himself here: we feel that he is a magnanimous and fair-minded man. At the end of the passage, Boaz's generosity comes out again when he sends Ruth back to Naomi loaded with barley. His refusal to allow her to return 'empty-handed' reverses Naomi's 'full-to-empty' lament in chapter 1. Naomi is keen to hear how the plan unfolded. She knows the kind of man that Boaz is and that he will act on the kinsman issue straight away.

5 The next-of-kin

Decisions were often made by the elders of a community at the city gate, and it is there that Boaz goes to find the aforementioned next-of-kin. With ten elders with him to sit in judgment, he explains the situation to the next-of-kin in rather different terms than the way it has actually occurred. He frames it in relation to a piece of land that Naomi has to sell, which had belonged to Elimelech, the one through whom the kinship relationship exists. The kinsman jumps at the chance to purchase the land, until Boaz reveals that with the field goes Ruth, the Moabitess. The man's excuse that he is worried about damaging his inheritance is probably a reference to Ruth's foreignness, but there may be other reasons for his rejection of the offer, which remain unsaid.

Verses 7–12 give an insight into the way transactions of this kind were carried out in ancient Israel, involving a ritual with a sandal. The next-of-kin, as a formalization of his intention to hand over the right to acquisition of the land and of Ruth, takes off his sandal. This is witnessed by the elders and by all assembled there (cf. 3:11, 'all the assembly of my people'). Boaz makes a proclamation of the transaction: he is now in receipt of all of Elimelech's legacy, including Ruth, who will become his wife.

The idea of continuing the name of the dead is found here. Remembrance and descendants are important themes in Israelite thought. As the people confirm the transaction, there is a reference to the matriarchs Rachel and Leah, both daughters of Laban and wives of Jacob (it is particularly interesting that the reference is to the women, not the men), who 'built up the house of Israel'—a reference to their twelve progeny (Genesis 29—30). This expresses the hope that the couple will have children.

The name Ephrathah appears in verse 11, meaning the region of Bethlehem. There is a second cross-reference in verse 12 to two patriarchs and a matriarch of Israel, this time to Tamar who bore a son, Perez, to Judah. She achieved this by posing as a prostitute, of whom Judah took his pleasure (Genesis 38): the parallel to the threshing floor comes to mind! These cross-references to other characters in the Old Testament are interesting as they show some inner-biblical exegesis going on within the canon itself.

6 David's great-grandmother!

Ruth 4:13–22

All we are left with now is the denouement. This, of course, has to involve the birth of a child, and it does: a son is born to Ruth at God's instigation.

The women of Bethlehem see this as the restoration of Naomi's kin. They pray that the boy's name will be great one day, but also that he will be a joy to Naomi in her old age. They also express Ruth's loyalty to Naomi, making it clear that the relationship between Ruth and Naomi is a two-way one: Ruth means a great deal to Naomi, 'more than seven sons' (v. 15). How marvellous that this favoured daughter-in-law is the mother of Naomi's new hope.

Oddly, the women of Bethlehem give the child a name. This was normally done by the child's mother. Is it another example of Ruth's submissiveness, that she gives her child over not just to Naomi but also to the wider female community to name? The name of the child is Obed, and a descendant only two generations away from him (i.e. his grandson) is none other than King David himself! This, of course, makes Ruth the Moabitess David's great-grandmother, in a surprising twist in the tale. The genealogies at the end of a book are often considered by scholars to be later additions and tedious at that, but in this case the genealogy holds the key to the reason that the story has been told in the first place. Ruth is a significant woman not just because she is a model of loyalty and good deeds, or because she is a convert to Yahwism. Her chief significance lies in her being the great-grandmother of the most famous king in Israel's history. From small agricultural origins come the powerful men who will lead Israel into its greatest period of united monarchy.

The book ends with a second, more detailed genealogy showing the link between Perez (born to Judah and Tamar) and Boaz, and on to David. It is made clear in this last genealogy that it is Boaz's line that is continuing, not just Elimelech's, through Naomi. And so the tale has been rounded off in a most satisfactory way, with God's gift of progeny being the channel of fresh blessing for all the characters involved. We hear nothing of Ruth's reaction—she once again takes a back seat—but she presumably feels fulfilled in remarriage to a caring husband, childbearing and true acceptance by the wider community.

Guidelines

Ruth sets us all an example of loyalty. The mother-in-law/daughter-in-law relationship can be close, but it can also have its strains. In this case, the main point of connection—Mahlon, Naomi's son—is dead and lost to them, so there is no real reason why Ruth should show such loyalty to Naomi. There is also a strong sense of community running through this text, with the elders, the assembly of the people and the townswomen all having their say. However, the family unit is a smaller unit within the wider community and both Naomi and Ruth are displaced persons, widows being in a difficult position in such a society with no husbands to protect them.

There are few references to God in this book, but we get the impression that he is constantly behind the scenes, directing the action. Much is made of good deeds, which are said to be rewarded by God, and the main characters call on God's name quite frequently. Ruth does so at the beginning when she swears her oath of loyalty to Naomi. Good outcomes (notably, the birth of Obed) are seen to come from God. This idea of God behind the scenes in our lives is a profound one: there is always a difficult tension between making decisions ourselves and relying on God to do so for us. Isaiah (see 30:15–16) chastised the people of his time for not trusting enough in God but instead relying too much on human insight. Proverbs 16:9 also puts it well: 'The human mind plans the way, but the Lord directs the steps.' There is a mysterious interaction here that is beyond our control, much as we would like to think that we direct the action.

Among many profound themes in this small book, one is about the acceptance of foreigners in the community. The Moabites were traditional enemies of Israel, and even Ruth's conversion didn't make her a complete insider. Sometimes parts of the Old Testament are seen as nationalistic: didn't Nehemiah condemn Hebrew men who married foreign wives (Nehemiah 13:23–27)? Yet this is just one strand, to which Ruth stands in opposition. The book shows an acceptance and a universalism lacking in other examples. The emphasis on good deeds (compare the emphasis in Proverbs on good behaviour leading to reward) indicates that anyone who is good, loyal and sincere, regardless of creed, race or colour, may be the recipient of God's blessings. We might do well to ponder this outlook as we interact with all types of people in today's very multicultural world.

FURTHER READING

K. Larkin, *Ruth and Esther*, Old Testament Guides, Sheffield Academic Press, 1996.
E. van Wolde, *Ruth and Naomi*, SPCK, 1997.
E.F. Campbell, *Ruth*, Anchor Bible 7, Doubleday, 1975.

EARTH KEEPING

'The way the universe *is* determines how man *ought* to behave himself in it' (Oliver O'Donovan, *Resurrection and Moral Order*).

Caring for creation is a neglected topic in some Christian circles and yet, in the face of global warming, we cry, 'How can we make the world a better place?' The average United Kingdom household emits 24.6 tons of carbon dioxide each year, approximately three times above a sustainable level. The long-term effects of diminishing world resources are hard to predict but they will certainly have a devastating impact globally and are already evidenced in the developing world. This threatens the stability of community and international relations as nations compete for decreasing global resources, threatening peace in the world.

In the last century, we saw a radical transformation of the human relation to nature. The optimistic belief that human progress (brought about through science, technology and the power of reason) would provide the utopian dream of a better world, without war and suffering, has not been realized. Are we really able to make the world a better place by ourselves?

The Christian message brings renewed meaning to the environmental concerns of our contemporary world and offers us a hope and a way of living well as God's earth-keepers. Throughout the Old and New Testaments, we see that God as Creator cares for everything he has made. He gives his creation order and meaning and sustains it through his own creative nature. These reflections will, I hope, remind us of the earthiness of the one who set the stars into space and is intimately involved in all that he has made. The Bible challenges our human-centred approach to God's promises of salvation and redemption and our domination of the earth's resources for our own ends.

Few people would want the world to go on exactly as it is. We recognize that there is something not quite right about our world. There is a dark side to life that we see in the face of injustice and poverty, greed, materialism and power. In the first week, we will turn to the pages of the Old Testament for guidance on environmental ethics. Then, in the second week, we will seek out the great wisdom about 'earth-keeping' to be found in the New Testament through Jesus' life, death and resurrection. Quotations are taken from the New International Version.

1 Creation and the gift of time

Genesis 1

The creation stories of Genesis 1 and 2 have been hotly debated in the scientific Age of Enlightenment. While these polemical debates over the big cosmological questions have made a valuable contribution to understanding our beginnings, to become over-embroiled in them can mean that we miss their relevance for our lives today. In *Caring for Creation* (BRF, 2005), Eugene Peterson claims that Genesis 1 and 2 are 'among the most uninterpreted and under-used texts for shaping an obedient and reverent life, following Jesus in our daily working and worshipping lives' (p. 20).

Dig deeper and read Genesis 1 aloud to discover the skilful and rhythmical arrangement of sets of words which Old Testament scholar Bruce Waltke calls the libretto for all of Israel's life. Like an opera or an oratorio, says Peterson, Genesis 1 expresses the creation rhythms in our language and work: we are created to live rhythmically. How does the rhythm work? Scholar Jon Leveson says that Genesis 1 makes it possible for us to access the creation rhythms through our personal involvement with the seventh day, the sabbath. The sabbath is the only creation action that God makes into a command:

Remember the Sabbath day by keeping it holy. Six days you shall labour and do all your work, but the seventh day is a Sabbath to the Lord your God. On it you shall not do any work... For in six days the Lord made the heavens and the earth, the sea, and all that is in them, but he rested on the seventh day. Therefore the Lord blessed the Sabbath day and made it holy. (Exodus 20:8–11)

When we remember the sabbath day and rest on it, we participate in the rhythm of creation and keep time with God. Eugene Peterson says,

'Keeping creation time preserves time as God's gift of holy rest; it erects a bastion in time against the commodification of time, reducing time to money or what we can get out of it, and having no time for beauty or anything that cannot be purchased or used' (pp. 23–24).

2 The glory of God

Psalm 19

As a child, I was captivated by two great books: Arthur Ransome's *Swallows and Amazons* and C.S. Lewis' *The Lion, the Witch and the Wardrobe*. Both books capture the imagination and hold me enthralled to this day. Beyond the text, the creativity and person of the writer resonates with the creativity and person of the reader.

Francis Bacon (1561–1626), a founder of the scientific method, saw the pursuit of scientific knowledge as being for the glory of God. He used the concept of God's two books—the book of his works and the book of his word. These two books hold together most beautifully in Psalm 19, which C.S. Lewis described as 'the greatest poem in the psalter and one of the greatest lyrics in the world'.

The two sections of the psalm represent Bacon's two 'books'. In the first section (vv. 1–6), God reveals himself in creation. God's glory is shouted out by the creation itself. The skies, including the sun, the moon and the stars, proclaim the work of his hands, all declaring the creativity and wonder of the artist. Creation witnesses to its Creator and praises its Creator. The glory of God is so powerful that it has no need for words, and yet we need to be sensitive enough to 'hear' the inaudible voice of the Creator. We need to be open to hear the voice that praises in the beauty of a sunset and the miracle of new birth—the echoes of a Creator God.

In the second section of the psalm (vv. 7–14), the psalmist emphasizes that the book of works is insufficient if we are to know God fully. Now the psalmist is delighting in the book of God's words, the Torah, the moral law. It is the book of God's words that transforms lives and leads to the knowledge of a loving and good God. Again, though, we must be careful not to deify the word. Biblical knowledge alone will not meet our needs. We need to engage with God's word as a living and vibrant revelation of himself, as spiritual food for our souls.

The final three verses encourage us to apply the word to our personal lives, actions, thoughts and words. In a world where God's rules are not followed and the Bible is unknown, Psalm 19 places both natural law and moral law alongside each other in the two books and asks for God's help for us as we try to keep in tune with his revelation.

3 Rejection of the Creator

Genesis 3:1–24

We approach this passage with thoughts of the chaos wrought by wars in the Middle East and the complexities surrounding them. The stories of inhumanity that frequently dominate the headlines leave us horrified by humankind's capacity for evil.

Here in Genesis 3 is an account of the reality and consequences of sin. It is the story of human rejection of the Creator God, and is not to be read with abstract, distant eyes and a purely intellectual approach. As commentator J. Walsh puts it, 'The sin depicted is not simply the first sin; it is all human sin; it is my sin. And I who hear the tale am forced to acknowledge that my sin too has cosmic dimensions; my sin too is an attack on creation and an establishment of moral chaos.'

The more symbolic than historical story is an account of the origin, reality and consequences of sin. As readers, we are asked to accept Adam and Eve as historical figures, but we also need to recognize the symbolism and see ourselves in Adam and Eve, asking how the account relates to practical questions of life.

The image of the serpent resonates with our Christian experience as we recognize the existence of a power beyond ourselves that tempts us into sin. Our weaknesses are known by this power, and this, we say, is the devil at work. The serpent misrepresents God by questioning what God has said about eating from the trees in the garden, and subtly changes the woman's understanding of the Creator and his abundant provision.

Yet sin is much more than a distorted understanding of God; it is a subtle luring and corrupting. It requires us to own the lies about God for ourselves and for us personally to reject God. In verses 2–3, the woman has distorted her understanding of God's generosity and misrepresents his words (compare 2:16–17). When we separate God's concern for all human beings from his desire for us to enjoy the goodness of creation, we open the door to selfishness. In the West, when we enjoy the goodness of great wealth and materialism, we do so frequently at the expense of those living in the developing world.

Desire and action are also involved in our rejection of God, as we read in verse 6, where sin is represented by the words 'saw', 'took', 'ate' and 'gave'. The woman's sin is an attempt to become like God. The reality of sin is a denial of our creatureliness, of the one who has given the gift of life and of our dependence on the goodness of our Creator.

In stark contrast to the provision of Genesis 2, the story of Genesis 3 shows the consequences of our rejection of God as the disruption of the created order and broken relationships with God, with ourselves and with creation itself. For the Christian, however, there is hope. When we read this passage in the light of the gospel, we can understand more fully the depth of our sin in the light of the cross of Christ. We can also experience the grace, mercy and forgiveness of the risen Lord who is God with us, the one who has delivered us from sin through the cross and resurrection.

4 God's covenant with the earth

Genesis 9

You know the story well: it begins in Genesis 6:5 with God outraged by human wickedness and sin. God decides to wipe humankind and every living creature from the face of the earth, resolving to make a fresh start with Noah and his family, who 'walked with God' and were obedient (6:9). God commands Noah to make an ark of cypress wood, giving him the exact dimensions for the vessel, and Noah carries out God's instructions. In 6:18 we read that God establishes a covenant with Noah and all his family. Noah is obedient and does everything that God commands him to do.

It is easy to read this Genesis story from a merely human perspective, but that would be to miss a crucial point. God's promise to Noah was a commitment to maintain the established relationship between Creator and creation. It is more than a story about the human condition, even though Noah and his family take centre stage. In Genesis 9, the promises of God for a future and a hope are for the whole of the created order. Old

Testament scholar Bruce Waltke points out that 'the intentional repetition of the phrases "every living creature" and "all life" eight times in verses 8–17 affirms God's desire to preserve every species. Therefore the human destruction of species must be a grave concern for God.'

In a world threatened by climate change and torn apart by war and environmental degradation, the promises of God should ring a note of hope for us today. At a time when over a quarter of the animal and plant species face extinction within 50 years, Noah's ark becomes a powerful symbol of God's command for human partnership with him in caring for all life and every living creature.

In the past, the value that we have placed on creation and life on earth has been related to our needs rather than the value that God placed on his creation, all of which he saw was good. The true value of other life on earth is established by the Creator who created and cared for it just as he did humankind. Therefore, it has an intrinsic value and is not just raw material for economic growth or to be subdued in the fight for survival.

Under the new covenant established through Christ, which is a fulfilment of the Old Testament covenants, we have the promise of redemption for all creation, forgiveness and new creation through the resurrection. How can we rediscover what the hope of this new covenant means for everyday living and restore the biblical place of all life and every living creature into our discipleship, as followers of Jesus who showed the way as the first earth-keeper?

5 The wisdom of God

Proverbs 8:22–36

Wisdom is personified as a woman in the Wisdom literature and is used to speak of justice and providence. In Proverbs 8 we read that wisdom is important to God the Creator: she is more precious than any precious metals or jewels. With wisdom are riches and honour, righteousness and justice. In the hymn of self-praise (vv. 22–31), wisdom speaks of creation and tells us three fundamental things.

In verse 22, we read that it was the Lord who 'brought forth' wisdom. God's intimate relationship with wisdom highlights the importance of wisdom to the Creator. Not only that, but wisdom was the firstborn of his works (v. 23), and thus the most valued of all the things God created.

Wisdom's pre-existence before the creation is made clear in verses 23–29. Wisdom was the 'craftsman' at the Creator's side (v. 30), co-creating with God. Therefore, she is fundamental to the whole creative process and to the universe, especially its sustainability and stability. Wisdom sets boundaries for the sea and contains the chaos of the world. Wisdom helps set the heavens in place and fixes the fountains of the deep. Wisdom sustains the order of God's creation and keeps chaos at bay.

Wisdom is also the source of joy and delight, so joy in human life is to be found in wisdom (v. 31). The appeal to listen to wisdom in the last verses—'for whoever finds me finds life and receives favour from the Lord'—brings together creation and righteous behaviour. If the ways of wisdom had been followed, would the earth be in the situation that it is now as a result of the destructive and greedy nature of fallen humankind?

6 A God of new possibilities

Isaiah 11:1–9

Walter Brueggeman, in his commentary on Isaiah, writes, 'This poem is about deep, radical, limitless transformation in which we—like lion, wolf and leopard—will have no hunger for injury, no need to devour, no yearning for brutal control, no passion for domination.' It is the biblical vision of *shalom*.

The prophet Isaiah announces Yahweh's rule coming to the earth through one on whom his Spirit rests, who brings deliverance for Israel and salvation for the whole of creation. It is a picture of God's plan for the whole earth and it calls us as partners in Christ to hold together four essential areas of Christian discipleship: delight in submission to God, justice for the poor, ecological peace, and the earth filled with the knowledge of God.

Delight in the fear of the Lord (vv. 2–3) is a characteristic of the king who is to come. This fear is a humble recognition of dependence on God and is a phrase that resonates throughout the Wisdom literature of Israel. Yahweh's anointed will not judge by appearances but will rule with righteousness, justice and faithfulness (vv. 4–5). Unlike the arrogant and oppressive rulers of Israel's history, this king will embody features of

Yahweh and will be concerned for the weak and the ones who have no voices.

In the final three verses, human *shalom* and the *shalom* of the earth are intertwined. These verses show a vision of a world where the curse of Eden has been removed, a time that creation has been waiting for with groans. The new kingdom ushered in by God will be a transformed world in which all that was lost through human sin will be restored and renewed. This is not only a vision for the restoration of humankind but for the whole of God's creation. What does it mean for us to celebrate the goodness of the natural world and, as followers of the Messiah, join with him in his integral mission on earth?

Guidelines

Go for a walk and reflect on your surroundings. How do the pictures around you reinforce your understanding of God as Creator?

29 OCTOBER–4 NOVEMBER

1 The Word became flesh

John 1:1–18

Jesus the Word shows us how important the creation is to God. Within these few verses lies a great affirmation of the physical creation as God literally 'pitches his tent with us' or, as NIV puts it, 'made his dwelling among us' (v. 14). He does not come to earth as some ethereal spiritual being, but as human flesh and blood. This presents a problem for most rationally minded people. How on earth does the Word become flesh? How does the Creator, God of the universe, become fully human?

However unbelievable the idea, the ancient world would have understood the meaning behind John's words in verse 14. In the Old Testament, Moses would speak to God face to face in the 'tent of meeting' (Exodus 33:7—34:35). John's revelation shows us that God has taken the initiative to enter into our world, which affirms not only our human nature but also the nature of this world. God's revelation is embedded in human experience situated in a particular time, place, culture and person. This shows us that human experience plays an important part in the unfolding history of God's creation.

Verses 9–10 prepare us for the entry of the Word into human existence: 'The true light… was coming into the world'. God chooses to send his Son into all the broken, rebellious sinfulness of the world to join with our humanity. As Paul puts it in Romans 5:8, 'God demonstrates his own love for us in this: While we were still sinners, Christ died for us.' We are important to God and, if humankind is so special to God, then so must the world be.

We cannot deny the physicality of Jesus. Platonic influences in Western Christianity have led to a denial of the material and physical world, which has encouraged a culture of use and abuse of the world's resources. Jesus affirms the earthiness of the physical and material world by becoming a part of it. Celtic theology finds the sacred in the earthiness of everyday life, tearing down the divide between the sacred and the secular, the spiritual and the material. When we encounter the Jesus of this world, he requires a response from us in order for us to know fully the nature of our Creator God.

2 Cosmic regeneration and restoration

Colossians 1:13–20

In his letter to the Colossian Christians, Paul is addressing important issues about Christ's sufficiency in response to their need to add extra religious rituals to the Christian life. We can use this passage to reflect on how Jesus is relevant to the questions of environmental crisis today.

Paul gives us the big picture in answer to questions about the nature of who Jesus is. Many scholars highlight the parallels that emphasize the Son of God's role in creation and new creation. They are significant because they show us that the same agent accomplishes both creation and new creation—that he is Lord of both creation and new creation. Paul argues that because Jesus is supreme in all things, he is also sufficient for all things. He is supreme in both creation and new creation.

- He is 'the image of the invisible God' (v. 15a) and 'the beginning' (v. 18b).

- He is 'the firstborn' of all creation (v. 15b) and from the dead (v. 18c).
- He is pre-eminent, as he is 'before all things' (v. 17a) and has supremacy 'in everything' (v. 18d).
- The Son unifies, as 'in him all things hold together' (v. 17b) and he 'reconciles... all things' (v. 20a).
- Everything is related to him in creation (v. 16b) and in new creation (v. 20c).

The redemption and reconciliation brought about by Jesus are not just for individual souls, but for 'all things, whether things on earth or things in heaven' (v. 20). The benefit and scope of Jesus' death on the cross and resurrection are for the salvation of individual sinners but also encompass a meaning beyond humankind, reaching into the whole cosmos. The one who sustains everything by his word will not abandon his creation but, out of love, will reconcile it to himself. The earth has a future and is safe because of God's redemptive purposes and divine actions in relation to the earth.

We need, in all things, to step back and get a bigger picture of God's restoration of his creation through Christ. Ultimately, God's salvation plan is to repair the damage done by sin and complete the restoration. It's a process that will eventually be completed, but in the meantime, are we prepared to follow the way? The way of salvation involves reducing the levels of pollutants and greenhouse gases, helping people overcome the spread of the AIDS virus, reducing the unpayable debt of developing countries and creating a just world economic system.

3 He does not live in temples built by hands
Acts 17:16–34

One of the issues surrounding environmental problems relates to community. For a global community to be sustainable, and if the world's resources are to be distributed equally among the people, the nations are required to work together for economic growth and development. They are also required to live at peace with one another in spite of their ethnic and cultural differences. It is not hard to see how we have failed to achieve anything close to a sustainable global community, and yet it is a necessary goal in today's world.

The great destroyer of community is exclusivity. The term 'ethnic cleansing' has crept into our vocabulary. Communities or nations 'cleanse' themselves of the others by driving out those who don't fit the criteria of the community. The land will then belong exclusively to those who have driven the others out. In today's passage, Paul is preaching in Athens. In verses 16–21, the people gathered are described by their ethnic and religious identities much as we would do today: these are exclusive groups who have their designated centres of community.

Paul addresses them and emphasizes the greatness and universality of God. He says that God is the Creator of all things, 'the world and everything in it' (v. 24). He is the source of all life (v. 28). He made every nation inhabiting the whole earth (v. 26). As the source and sustainer of life, he is personal and wants to be in relationship with all people (vv. 27–28). He calls all people to repent (v. 30). And all of this is seen most clearly in the life, death and resurrection of his Son, Jesus Christ (v. 31).

Paul does not address the gathered community in the synagogue, as we might expect. He is out in the marketplace. He recognizes that before he belongs to the community of the faithful believers, he belongs to the universal community of God's created humanity. Our community, first and foremost, is the created community in which all were fearfully, wonderfully and uniquely made in God's image. Paul understood that there was no place in which Jesus was not and could not be relevant.

The gospel message is not communicated in a disembodied word but through the Word made flesh. It is good to remember that Christ first embraced the other through his love and acceptance. Likewise, we are placed in particular communities in order to embrace the other—not, as we so often do, to build or choose an exclusive church community of like-minded, compatible people. If we are going to build a global sustainable community, we may need to take up the challenge to embrace both the universal and particular in community.

4 Liberation

Romans 8:18–30

Paul recognizes that our human destiny is bound up with that of the world, and our resurrection will involve our joining in with God's new creation of all he has created. This passage questions the human-centric and individualistic view of the bodily resurrection. Paul is reflecting the Jewish idea that history is dependent on the purposes of God being worked out from creation through to consummation, and he links this with Christ's identity as the creator and consummator.

The creation itself waits in eager expectation for the revelation of the glory that is to come (v. 19). Here, Paul personifies creation in order to describe it. In the Old Testament, the personification of nature is used to see creation pointing towards the glory of the Creator God (see, for example, Psalm 19:1). Paul interprets the sufferings of this world as sharing in the sufferings of Christ, which is part of sharing in his glory. We are not promised a life free of suffering, and must come to terms with the fact that suffering is a reality in this world. However, our suffering, Paul says, should be seen in the light of the future. There is a time of healing, hope and justice.

Paul sees creation as an important component in pointing toward the new creation. Creation has value and God is working his purposes out through his creation. Creation has been subjected to frustration as a result of the broken relationships between God, humankind and nature. Creation is caught up in the fall as a consequence of human sin. The hope for creation is that creation will be liberated to be what God wants it to be (v. 21).

The hope for the future is not a disembodied spirit world but a new creation (vv. 24–25). The Spirit groans along with creation and the believer, and helps believers in their weakness (vv. 26–27). The initiative is God's. God is working his purposes out, and our hope for the future is based on God's action. The Spirit propels us to take seriously the frustration and groaning of this world and compels us to join with God in working out his new creation purposes.

5 A new heaven and new earth

2 Peter 3:3–16

There are many cosmological conjectures today about the future of the universe. The beliefs that a person holds about the future of the earth will shape and affect their ethical attitude towards the planet: if we believe that humankind is the centre of existence and the earth has no intrinsic value in itself, then we will milk it for all its worth.

There are contrasting images in the Bible of transience and preservation when describing the future of the earth, from the idealistic image of the new heavens and new earth in Isaiah 65:17–25 to Peter's dramatic presentation in our passage today. This passage that has led to confusion about the future destiny of the planet, because of poor translations. The overall image is clear: here we have an act of God with a radical effect on the universe. If we examine the text in its context, however, we can see that the passage is about God's cleansing judgment, whereby evil is destroyed and creation purified, rather than the destruction of this present creation. In verses 10 and 12, the 'elements' that are destroyed are the distorted powers that have thwarted God's rule on earth. The context emphasizes the scrutiny of human deeds, which makes sense of Peter's question, 'What kind of people ought you to be?' (v. 11). When Peter talks about the new heaven and new earth, it has to do with morality—that is, a realm in which righteousness is at home (v. 13).

The future of humankind and the earth are entwined in God's redemptive purposes. The judgment is that of a loving God who will restore and redeem his broken world and who brings hope to the planet in the form of a restored, harmonious creation—God's kingdom on earth as it is in heaven.

6 Jesus and the resurrection

Luke 24:13–35

Yesterday we reflected on the future of the universe and God's plan of restoration. The catalyst for the continuity of creation and new creation, new heaven and new earth, is centred on the death and resurrection of Jesus. The witness of the disciples on the road to Emmaus was a single event that changed humble fishermen into international heroes and martyrs, and transformed their relationship to the world they lived in.

On the road, Jesus went through the story from Genesis to Chronicles (the last book in the Hebrew scriptures), showing that, in order to bring in God's new creation, he had to suffer, die and rise again (v. 27). The resurrection is an affirmation by God of the material world. In order to put an end to the domination of death and destruction, Christ, through God, must be greater than nature. The resurrection is a correction to the whole created order, an abolition within nature of death, corruption and decay.

In the same way today, we witness to the truth of the resurrection of Jesus as we reveal its transforming nature in our lives and in our relationships with one another. The passages that we have looked at over the past two weeks teach us some central truths about God's plan and purposes for the future of the earth and should enable us to make a positive contribution to the environmental debate. As Christians, we can accept the cosmic judgment that Jesus promised but we do not need to accept the pessimism that exists in the environmental movement today. Our hope comes from the certainty that we have of God's final restoration of all that he has made. In the meantime, he calls us to be earth-keepers, stewards and co-creators with him.

Guidelines

Reflect on these words: 'Thy will be done on earth as it is in heaven.' Ask yourself how concerned you are for the future of the earth. What was Jesus' attitude to the earth? How might the Church become more environmentally responsible?

FURTHER READING

Ghillean Prance, *The Earth Under Threat: A Christian Perspective*, Wild Goose Publications, 1996.

Ed. Sarah Tillett, *Caring for Creation: Biblical and Theological Perspectives*, BRF, 2005

David Wilkinson, *The Message of Creation*, BST, 2002.

James Jones, *Jesus and the Earth*, SPCK, 2003.

W. Brueggeman, *Isaiah 1—39*, John Knox, 1998.

Alastair McIntosh, *Soil and Soul*, Aurum Press Ltd, 2002.

2 CHRONICLES

2 Chronicles takes up the story where 1 Chronicles leaves off (see *Guidelines* September–December 2005). They are one book. The Chronicler wrote not primarily to record the past but to encourage and challenge his contemporaries in the small Judean community centred on Jerusalem in the post-exilic period, about the fourth century BC. With past glory long since gone, they were subjects of the Persian empire, but the Chronicler courageously affirms their continuity with past centuries. They are still God's people, still representative of his kingdom on earth, and he is still their God, active in history. There are lessons to be learned from that history, about human responsibility and God's power to save. Prophets bearing God's word to king and people figure frequently in the narrative, reminding the Chronicler's readers over the centuries, including us today, of the need to pay heed to the word of the Lord. There is nothing narrowly nationalistic about the story. Judah, like the nations, stands under judgment. Destiny for good or ill lies with freedom of choice, and in God's mercy repentance is always possible.

The narrative is interesting, too, in showing how later generations applied the ancient traditions to their own times. Circumstances had changed since the days of which the Chronicler tells. Their status as an independent nation was over, but as God's people it was still their obligation to offer him worship and obedience. A diminished people did not mean a diminished God. The Chronicler's apparently rigid view of reward and punishment seems simplistic to us, but he leaves room always for God's mercy. His insistence on accountability also challenges us and our society lest we slip into the tragic situation with which the book of Judges ends: 'everyone did what was right in their own eyes'.

Like 1 Chronicles, this narrative is not all easy reading. We must read patiently and perceptively, opening our minds to God, accepting the challenge, and we shall not go away empty.

The Bible version on which the notes are based is the NRSV.

1 Equipped for the task in hand

2 Chronicles 1:1–17

Everything Solomon does is on a grand scale. His worship (vv. 2–6), his wisdom (vv. 7–13) and his wealth (vv. 14–17) are all beyond the ordinary. Yet there is a surprising touch of humility. He recognizes before God his inadequacy: 'Who can rule this great people of yours?' (v. 10). The task is held in trust for God.

The story starts in Gibeon, a prominent sanctuary where David too had worshipped. Here stood the ancient 'tent of meeting' ('the tent of God's presence', NEB) from wilderness days. By chapter 5, Solomon has transferred it to Jerusalem where David had already installed the ark (v. 4). Thereafter the focus is on Jerusalem.

Times have changed since David came to the throne. They were times of hardship, of hostility and struggle for power. Solomon's accession (1 Chronicles 29:22) seems altogether smoother. Yet there were divided loyalties (does the word 'established' in verse l hint at this?) which broke out under his successor, Rehoboam. The story in 1 Kings 1—2 of intrigues to ensure Solomon's succession gives a different picture, a reminder that Chronicles is supplementary to Kings and written for a different and later situation.

The Chronicler's interest in worship, a recurrent theme throughout, is immediately evident. Solomon's first recorded action (v. 6) is a public celebration of worship with 'the whole assembly'. A comparison with the parallel narrative in 1 Kings 3 throws another interesting light on the Chronicler's different perspective. There Solomon demonstrates his God-given wisdom by resolving the tricky situation of two prostitutes both claiming the same baby, but the Chronicler has fewer human interest stories. For him, Solomon's wisdom and wealth are demonstrated in building the Lord's temple (and his own palace), an account that follows immediately in 2:1.

Let the Chronicler's emphasis on worship challenge us: how central to my life is worship, public or private?

2 For the Lord, nothing but the best

2 Chronicles 2:1–18

Here and in 8:1, Solomon's palace is linked with the building of the temple, a house for 'the name of the Lord' and for the king. Before we condemn this association as arrogance on Solomon's part, we do well to recall that in ancient Israel (we are now with Solomon in the tenth century BC) the king was regarded as the agent of God's rule on earth. At best, this meant delivering God's justice in an unjust world. We see this most clearly in the Psalms. God is 'mighty King, lover of justice' (Psalm 99:4) and the reigning king is to reflect this on earth—a high ideal not often attained. Significantly, the only psalm attributed to Solomon (Psalm 72) is a prayer for justice, with the emphasis on the poor, the needy and the oppressed. The Chronicler gives no detail of the royal palace, unlike the extensive description in 1 Kings 7:1–12.

The theology of the temple is worth reflecting on. Not in any crudely restrictive sense was it regarded as God's dwelling place: 'heaven, even highest heaven, cannot contain him. Who am I to build a house for him, except as a place to make offerings?' (v. 6). Only the best of natural resources and human skill is good enough. Phoenicians from Tyre are to share in its construction. (A 'bath' is approximately 22 litres, a 'kor' ten times as much.) There is nothing racist here. Huram-abi, the man in charge of the work, is of mixed parentage, Israelite and Tyrian.

Comparison with the account in 1 Kings 5 is interesting. There (v. 7), Hiram king of Tyre praises Solomon's God-given wisdom. The Chronicler enlarges on it with Hiram's recognition of God as Creator. Although there is less explicit criticism of Solomon than in 1 Kings 1—2 and 11:1–40, some harsh realities of his reign begin to emerge. The resident foreigners (*gerim*, without citizens' rights) were conscripted, with overseers 'to make the people work' (v. 18). This is forced labour in all but name, though less explicit than in 1 Kings 5:14, where the word used (*mas*) refers specifically to forced labour.

'What shall I return to the Lord for all his bounty to me?' (Psalm 116:12).

3 Worship, music and mystery

2 Chronicles 5:1–14

The climax of Solomon's building comes with the dedication of the temple and the installing of the ark. The difference between this account and the parallel in 1 Kings 8 illustrates the Chronicler's particular interest in liturgy. After only a brief mention of the sacrificial rituals, he directs attention to the worship and music (verse 13 quotes Psalm 136:1), emphasizing not only the magnificent celebration but also the sense of joyful unity, the priests without regard to their divisions, the musicians and singers in unison. The occasion is the great autumn festival, the feast of Tabernacles/Booths, reminding Israel of its wilderness journeys from slavery to freedom (Leviticus 23:42–43). The Chronicler's description gives pride of place to the ark, which held the tablets of the covenant made on Mount Sinai, symbolizing God's commitment to his people and the obligation upon them to obey the commandments out of gratitude to him for their deliverance from slavery.

The chapter ends in mystery. The temple and its magnificent dedication can be described in human terms, but the presence of the transcendent Lord in the midst of his people is indescribable. It is mystery shrouded in cloud, concealing yet revealing the glory of the Lord. So overwhelming was the sense of his presence that the priests were swept off their feet, unable to stand and minister before him. This sense of the awesome hiddenness of God continues into 6:1 (see also Exodus 40:34–38). 'Cloud' as symbolic of the divine presence is a recurring motif in both the Old and the New Testament. Among these instances can be cited the making of the covenant on Mount Sinai (Deuteronomy 5:22) and, in the New Testament, both the transfiguration and the ascension. Two contrasting verses come to mind: '[He] dwells in unapproachable light, whom no one has ever seen or can see' (1 Timothy 6:16) and 'But we do see Jesus…' (Hebrews 2:9).

4 The Lord who hears and answers prayer

2 Chronicles 6:18–21, 28—7:1

Solomon's magnificent prayer repays careful study. Its focus is certainly the earthly temple, the symbol of God's presence, but it should be understood throughout in the light of verse 18: 'Even heaven and the highest heaven cannot contain you, how much less this house that I have built!' The ultimate question is posed: 'Will God indeed reside with mortals on earth?' For us who live in the light of the incarnation, the answer can only be 'yes'—and now, after the ascension, we have dwelling with us and in us that other 'Comforter/Advocate', the Holy Spirit (John 14:16).

The emphasis on prayer and the absence of any reference to sacrifice suggest that the passage may have originated in this form during the exile in Babylon, when there was no access to temple sacrifices. Be that as it may, in the Chronicler's time, although the community itself was centred on the temple with its sacrificial rituals, there were many Jews still scattered in the diaspora for whom prayer was the sole means of approach to God.

The breadth of the prayer is impressive. It embraces justice, repentance and forgiveness. It is also realistic: 'there is no one who does not sin' (v. 36). But from God no secrets are hidden and he already knows the human heart (v. 30). Nor is he a narrowly nationalistic God. His mercy extends to all, native-born Israelite and foreigner alike (vv. 32–33).

The Chronicler's simplistic view of reward and punishment (vv. 36–39) is not one that we can adopt. The book of Job in the Old Testament and the words of Jesus in the New (Luke 13:1–4) are a strong protest against that rigid equation of suffering with sin, but the Chronicler knew, as we do, an endlessly forgiving God. Solomon's prayer is a salutary reminder to us of God's transcendence, of his awesome power and mercy. He is not a God who can be domesticated, as if he were merely humanity writ large, but he is the Lord Almighty.

5 The Lord's response to Solomon's prayer

2 Chronicles 7:2–6, 12–22

Solomon's great prayer evoked an awesome response: God's presence manifest in fire and glory! And the result for the congregation was joyful worship and thanksgiving with musical accompaniment—a recurring interest, as we have seen, to the Chronicler. Despite the dangers and demands of life, the worshippers hold to the central truth that 'his steadfast love (hesed) endures for ever' (v. 3). Hesed is an interesting Hebrew word and no single English term sufficiently represents its meaning. It signifies love, kindness, mercy and loyalty both of humans and, supremely, of the Lord. Sadly, Israel's loyalty was often short-lived. Hosea likens it to early morning dew, so quickly dissipated (Hosea 6:4).

God is a forgiving God but human accountability is also emphasized. There is to be not only prayer but also true repentance (v. 14). The Chronicler doesn't shrink from anthropomorphisms, portraying the Almighty in human terms. His is an interventionist God whose ears, eyes and heart (vv. 15–16) are attuned to his people. Yet there is a 'But...' (v. 19): God never condones sin. The root of the sin depicted here is ingratitude, the failure to remember the Lord's past mercies (v. 22)—a hard-hitting challenge to us who have known yet greater mercies through Jesus the Saviour.

The forgiving God is not to be trifled with. His steadfast love is within reach but we ourselves can make it unavailable (verse 19 is in the plural, addressed to all the people). The fact that disaster was understood not in terms of the Lord's weakness but of his strength ('Why has the Lord done such a thing?' v. 21) is highly significant. To us, the Chronicler's interpretation of history often seems simplistic but, for Israel, whether in exile or in later difficult days, it was, strangely, a word of hope. The Lord himself was in the situation and in this lay encouragement for the future. This God, who held his people accountable, could also save. This is our God.

6 The great schism

2 Chronicles 9:31—10:19

The queen of Sheba, from south-west Arabia, astonished at Solomon's wealth and wisdom, drew an unwarranted conclusion: 'Happy are your people!' (9:7). This is ironical in view of what is to follow. Chapter 10 is an altogether sadder story. Solomon's death makes way for a new king, his son Rehoboam, and a new and tragic period in the nation's life. The idealized picture of Solomon's reign gives way to a more realistic one. If Solomon was famed for his wisdom, Rehoboam's epitaph is folly. He ignores the king's obligation to secure justice for his people (see Psalm 72) and plays into the hands of his rival Jeroboam. From then on, Israel in the north and Judah in the south diverge, sometimes at peace, sometimes hostile. Latent tensions between northern and southern tribes, which had been simmering under the surface even during David's reign (2 Samuel 20:1), now break out. Schism has become a reality (c.930BC). From here onwards, the Chronicler's interest lies with Judah, the forerunner of his own community, and with the northern kingdom Israel only when it impinges on Judah.

The Chronicler has painted a glowing picture of Solomon compared with that in 1 Kings 11:1–8. Yet we have seen hints already that Solomon's building ambitions bore heavily on some sections of society, not only foreigners (2 Chronicles 2:17–18; 8:7–8) but citizens too: hence the urgent plea to Rehoboam for relief from the burdens (10:4). A rival leader, Jeroboam, was already in waiting, encouraged by the prophet Ahijah. To discover Ahijah's words, we need to go to 1 Kings 11:29–32. The omission in Chronicles of so significant a prophetic word is further evidence that the Chronicler intended his writings to be read in the light of the earlier traditions. Thereafter, the parallel, often tragic, stories of Judah and Israel after the schism illustrate Rehoboam's folly:

- his arrogance.
- his insincerity in asking advice merely to bolster his own inclinations.
- his neglect of the obligation to help the oppressed.

And what of us, God's people today?

Guidelines

For most of this week, the narrative has focused on Solomon, but with his son Rehoboam a downward spiral begins. The fragile unity between Israel and Judah, maintained throughout two long reigns, is now finally ruptured, never in history to be fully restored.

The Chronicler, writing close on 500 years after Solomon in dramatically changed circumstances both politically and socially, has a message from history for his own contemporaries. Both challenge and encouragement are found in the stories he retells, but he offers no comfortable, easy security in a nationalistic God. This is the Lord Almighty, and king and people alike are accountable before him. But always there is 'a way back to God from the dark paths of sin'. God is a forgiving God with 'eyes, ears and heart' attentive to his people's prayers—and so the Chronicler revels in worship and music as a fitting response to the Lord's goodness and his revealed glory.

1 The perils of success

2 Chronicles 12:1–16

Rehoboam's is a sad story. The Chronicler, with greater detail than the brief account in 1 Kings 14, draws out lessons for his contemporaries: the community must set the Lord and his will at the centre of their life. It was not so with Rehoboam. For three years, all was well. Priests and Levites 'who had set their hearts to seek the Lord' (11:16–17) came to Jerusalem from all the tribes. Rehoboam flourished, but it was not to last. Notice the ominous words of 12:1: 'was established... grew strong... abandoned the law of the Lord'. The one whose role was to represent God's kingdom on earth had failed, and 'all Israel with him'.

It was Rehoboam's arrogance that provoked the schism between north and south. Simmering discontentment burst into the open. Then, in the Chronicler's scheme of things, unfaithfulness to the Lord brought disaster. Shishak/Shoshenq of Egypt invaded c.926BC. His victories are recorded in the great temple of Amun in Karnak. Significantly, Jerusalem is not listed among his conquests: the city was spared, the Chronicler tells us, at the cost of its temple and palace treasures (v. 9). But the fortified cities with which Rehoboam had surrounded the Judean heartland (11:6–11) were captured —a reminder of the frailty of all human defence. Disaster had come quickly in Rehoboam's fifth year but the lesson was not learnt. His reign is encapsulated in verse 14: 'He did evil, for he did not set his heart to seek the Lord.'

Two notable themes in Chronicles recur here: the need for humility and for loyalty. Verse 8 merits reflection. To turn from serving the Lord brings not freedom but servitude. An ancient story, this, but it is as challenging today as in the Chronicler's time. Where do our loyalties lie? Human self-sufficiency that dispenses with reliance on the Lord can end only in futility.

2 Destructive anger

2 Chronicles 15

The story of Rehoboam's son, Abijah, comes in chapter 13. In today's reading, we are in the reign of Asa, Rehoboam's grandson. Both are viewed more favourably than Rehoboam, yet the chronicler is not entirely consistent. Despite his unqualified approval of Asa—'[his] heart… was true all his days' (v. 17)—there is a negative side to the story in 16:9–10. Both chapters highlight the important role of prophets in bringing God's word to bear in challenging the king: first Azariah, then Hanani (16:7). Prophets were charismatic figures, dependent on the spirit/breath of God, not swayed by the monarch's favour. Asa readily accepted Azariah's encouragement (15:8), but it was a different matter when Hanani criticized him: anger, injustice, rage, cruelty, a mounting crescendo of evil (16:9–10).

We usually associate priests with sacrifice, but they had another vital role, that of teaching. Verses 3–4 are a salutary reminder of what can happen when leaders fail in their God-given task. In the period of the judges, anarchy prevailed and the leaderless people 'did what was right in their own eyes' (Judges 21:25). Sacrifice, of itself, is not enough. God cannot be manipulated by ritual niceties. He requires of his worshippers nothing less than heart commitment. They made a covenant to seek the Lord 'with all their heart and with all their soul' (v. 12) and 'with their whole desire' (v. 15). The result was rejoicing: 'and he was found by them'.

For Asa, family relationships had to take second place. The asherah, symbol of a Canaanite goddess, meant divided loyalties. A rare word is used of the image, literally 'a horrid thing' (*mipletset*), associated with the verb 'to shudder'. The quality of leadership under God, prophetic and priestly, resulted in attractive witness. Great numbers from the northern kingdom rejoined Judah when they saw that 'the Lord his God was with [Asa]' (v. 9). Sadly, among these bracing words verse 13 brings us up short, a reminder of the discontinuity between the Old and New Testaments. The Chronicler's sermon speaks powerfully to us about true leadership and its result, effective witness. But history—recent history, too—warns of the disastrous consequences of intolerance. Judah was struggling, in Asa's and in the Chronicler's time, for survival in a threatening world. Our struggle is not against flesh and blood (Ephesians 6:12).

3 A tale of two prophets

2 Chronicles 18:1–13, 16–27

There is now a time of collaboration between north and south, after the hostility of 16:1. It remains a mystery why Jehoshaphat, in a strong position militarily with forces in the fortified cities protecting Judah's borders (17:2, 12–13), made an alliance with Ahab, the great enemy of Elijah and promoter of Baal worship in the heart of the northern kingdom (1 Kings 16:31–33; 18:17–18). Marriage alliances had been Solomon's undoing, and so it is here. Clearly Jehoshaphat has doubts about the military alliance. Does he try to backtrack from over-ready compliance? Twice he seeks guidance from the Lord.

The story of the two prophets, Zedekiah and Micaiah, is illuminating, one reinforcing the congratulatory message of the mass of prophets, the other standing in courageous isolation, and suffering for it. Two themes interweave: the one against the many (compare Elijah on Mount Carmel, 1 Kings 18) and the monarch who prefers adulation to truth. What makes a true prophet? According to this passage, it is the one who stands in the Lord's presence, listening to his word. Zedekiah is more flamboyant, with his dramatic symbolic action (v. 10). What was Micaiah's source of courage? The contrast between verses 9 and 18 is surely not accidental. 'The Lord sitting on his throne' (v. 18) echoes verse 9, where we see two royally robed kings 'sitting on their thrones'. Here is divine majesty versus earthly kingship.

Ahab wants truth from Micaiah, but truth that is favourable—the perennial temptation to pray for guidance that suits our intentions. The story is couched in thought-forms that are alien to us: the Lord sends a lying spirit (v. 21). But Chronicles, for all its remoteness from our world, reflects human nature. Micaiah, courageous and loyal, fades from the scene, his fate unrecorded. Ahab's strategem to overturn the word of the Lord fails: 'at sunset he died' (v. 34). Human manoeuvres cannot nullify God's will.

This is a challenging story. Do I sometimes go with the tide, the popular voice? Do I seek divine approval for what I have already determined?

4 Singing in the eye of the storm

2 Chronicles 20:13–33

This chapter contrasts with yesterday's reading. There Jehoshaphat was confident, seeking God's guidance from a position of strength. Now comes a low point, a time of weakness and fear. Yet this, too, is a story of deliverance. In it the Chronicler finds a salutary lesson for his contemporaries, for this is not history retold for its own sake but with a theological, converting purpose.

Two verses in particular repay careful reflection. Jehoshaphat channels his weakness and perplexity into prayer (v. 12). In response comes the assurance of the Lord's presence at the heart of danger (v. 17). Leave room for God to act: he is in control—a sentiment close to Isaiah 7:4 and meaningful to us whatever our circumstances, whether they be spiritual or physical dangers. Judah's anxiety, gathering together its babies, wives and children, reflects the peril for helpless families in Dafur today. The ancient words have modern echoes.

The Lord chooses whom he wills to bear his message—not a prophet this time but a Levite inspired by his Spirit. His words remind the people of past triumphs of weakness versus military might, events well known to the Chronicler's readers, versed as they were in the ancient traditions. There are echoes of David versus Goliath (v. 15; 1 Samuel 17:47), of Moses faced with Pharaoh's army at the Red Sea (v. 17; Exodus 14:13–14), and of Ahaz terrified by hostile forces (v. 20; see Isaiah 7:9).

Here once again we face the continuity and the discontinuity of Old and New Testaments. The words are a powerful challenge to us in times of weakness and uncertainty, although 'our struggle is not against enemies of blood and flesh, but… against the spiritual forces of evil' (Ephesians 6:12). There is strength for us here, not only in spiritual battles but in the stresses and uncertainties of everyday life: 'stand still, and see the victory of the Lord on your behalf' (v. 17). We, too, can look beyond the immediate to a greater reality, acknowledging in humility his strength. And we, too, can rejoice in his steadfast love (*hesed*) even in the eye of the storm.

5 Gross ingratitude

2 Chronicles 24:1–22

The previous chapters tell of coup and counter-coup. Athaliah, who seized the throne by ruthless murder, herself met a violent death. Seven-year-old Joash succeeded to the throne. Under the wise guidance of the priest Jehoiada, all went well. The temple was restored and worship purified after Athaliah's depredations. Her condemnation, though brief, is absolute:

'that wicked woman' (v. 7) is a milder expression than the Hebrew, which is more literally 'the (embodied) wickedness'. But an ominous note sounds already in Joash's story (vv. 2, 14). All is well while the faithful priest is the king's counsellor, but Joash is easily swayed.

The practical details of the orderly raising of funds for the temple's restoration are interesting. Joash seems to have invented a thief-proof collecting chest. (Is there a suspicion of dishonesty in 2 Kings 12:7?) The restoration, despite the imposition of taxes on the people, brought them joy, and what had gone wrong under Athaliah was put right.

Inevitably, the wise influence of the faithful priest Jehoiada was eventually removed by death, and others got the king's ear. The young Joash, with eager enthusiasm, had restored the temple and its worship (note the rare criticism of the Levites, v. 5); sadly, the older Joash was implicit in reinstating idol worship (v. 17), a timely reminder that past achievements are no guarantee of the future.

Worse was to come. Prophets were ignored and Jehoiada's own son, Zechariah, was rejected and stoned to death. (His murder is referred to in Matthew 23:35, Chronicles being the last book in the Hebrew Bible). The monumental ingratitude of this slaughter is clear from 22:11, where we see that Joash, as a seven-year-old, owed his life to Jehoiada's wife. Finally, Joash's downfall is complete, as he is killed by two of his own servants. Jehoiada the priest is rightly the hero of the story. With his royal connections (22:11) he received burial among Judah's kings. Not so Joash (24:25).

6 Above all things, stay faithful to the Lord

2 Chronicles 26:1–23

Joash was succeeded by his son Amaziah—another story of disaster after a promising start, ending in conspiracy and regicide (25:27). More famous, though, is Amaziah's son Uzziah. Isaiah's great temple vision and subsequent call to be a prophet are dated in the year of Uzziah's death (Isaiah 6:1). His was a prosperous reign, helped by the fact that at this period (early 8th century), Syria was weak and the two powerful nations, Assyria and Egypt, were without territorial ambitions. So Uzziah flourished, renowned not only for military strength and the building of fortifications but also for his love of the soil (v. 10). A possible link has been suggested between his towers in the wilderness and Qumran, the site of the discovery of the Dead Sea scrolls. Yet here, too, pride was his undoing: strength… pride… destruction, a recurrent theme in Chronicles. 'He was false (*ma'al*) to the Lord his God' (v. 16); 'you have done wrong (*ma'al*)' (v. 18).

The king was not an absolute monarch. Like the humblest of his people, he was subject to God's law. In pre-exilic times, especially at festivals, the king seems to have had a leading part in liturgical worship. Here, Uzziah's real offence seems to have been the attempt to burn incense on the altar of incense located in the most sacred part of the temple. The priests had courage: history, even the recent past, had shown all too often the fate by summary execution of those who opposed the monarch (see, for example, 24:21). But faithfulness to the Lord outweighed their personal safety. Uzziah's high-handed action had been intrusive, overstepping the boundaries. Now he was excluded not only in life but in death (vv. 21, 23).

Uzziah's story has parallels to that of Joash. Both had a wise and supportive counsellor in their early days. Both failed in the long run to stay the course, Joash by weakly condoning idol worship, Uzziah by arrogantly usurping the priestly role. The account of Uzziah's reign in Kings is brief (there he is called Azariah: 2 Kings 15:1–7). The Chronicler, with access to other sources, drew out a powerful lesson for his own time: above all things, stay faithful to the Lord!

Guidelines

One thing that Chronicles has warned against repeatedly in this week's readings is the peril that lurks behind success. Time after time, things began well and ended badly because with success came pride and complacency. One of the words used frequently to describe the cause of this downward slide is *ma'al*, which means 'unfaithfulness', shortchanging the Lord. Poor leadership led the nation into disaster—like king, like people. Yet they, too, were accountable before God. Theirs was not a national god whose fortunes were bound up with his people's, to be coerced by ritual acts and the externals of worship. He was and is the Lord God who desires commitment with one's whole heart and soul. The result of such commitment is joy and gladness, worship from overflowing hearts even in the eye of the storm.

1 Ahaz and his questionable theology

2 Chronicles 28:1–5, 9–15, 22–27

Here is a surprise! The Chronicler presents an extraordinarily positive portrayal of the northern kingdom, which, for the most part, lies outside his remit. Israel, the northern kingdom, enters into the Chronicler's account only when it impinges on the situation in Judah, the southern kingdom. This emphasis is not motivated by prejudice against the north, as is evident from today's account of the most extraordinary magnanimity and compassion shown by Israel to the defeated Judean captives in their hour of need (vv. 12–15): this is truly a high point in the narrative.

Ahaz, in contrast, sinks to a new low, not only encouraging Baal worship but engaging in appalling rituals (v. 3). Whether he made his sons pass through fire (NRSV) or sacrificed his sons in the fire (NIV), it was an objectionable practice, unacceptable to the worship of Yahweh. The making of Baal images was a blatant rejection of the first two of the Ten Commandments. Ahaz closed down even the Jerusalem temple, replacing it with altars in all corners of the city and throughout Judah (vv. 24–25), and all of this was the result of ignorance and unsound theology: 'Because the gods of the kings of Aram helped them, I will sacrifice to them so that they may help me' (v. 23). What a pathetic statement of a despairing man—and he Judah's king, representative of God's reign on earth!

Yet the remarkable passage in verses 13–15 relieves the gloom. We have no historical evidence for this generous action but it can hardly be an invention of the Chronicler. Once again, the intervention of a prophet, this time in the northern kingdom, is pivotal. There were still some who paid attention to the word of the Lord. The Chronicler is obviously not narrowly nationalistic in his concentration on Judah. His own post-exilic circumstances in the small, struggling Judean community dictated this focus. The northern kingdom outshines Judah in its compassionate generosity to its erstwhile enemies (v. 15), a foreshadowing of the good Samaritan in Luke.

Ahaz tried to buy himself out of danger, 'but it did not help him' (v. 21). We have seen how prosperity turned some from the Lord and distress brought them back. Not so with Ahaz. Distress only increased his unfaithfulness (vv. 19, 22). With the temple closed and Baal altars everywhere, it looked like the end of faithful worship in Jerusalem, but with the living God there is always hope and a new beginning. Ahaz's son was Hezekiah, to whose reforms the next four chapters are dedicated.

2 Hezekiah's reforms

2 Chronicles 29:1–11; 30:1–5, 18–21

Hezekiah was enthusiastic. In the first month of his first year, the temple was reopened and worship restored as the focus of national life. Nothing was to be treated casually or negligently. To stand and minister in the Lord's presence was a solemn obligation (29:11). Today's readings are a good illustration that Chronicles is not merely a repetition of Kings but has its own perspective. Thus 29:1–2 is parallel to 2 Kings 18:2–3 but the religious reforms, so extensively described in Chronicles, are passed over in one verse in 2 Kings 18:4.

Passover had been a family festival, as it is in Judaism today. Hezekiah made it a central, national festival. An open invitation to the northern kingdom to share in the festival met with scorn (30:10–11): only a few were humble enough to join in. Was the Chronicler perhaps hoping for the eventual restoration of unity between north and south, a renewal of the former Davidic kingdom? It happened to some small extent under Hezekiah. Maybe it could happen again.

We often think of the Old Testament as a book of strict rules and unbending regulations for worship, but here are two fascinating instances of flexibility to meet exceptional circumstances. The celebration of Passover, traditionally held in the first month, was delayed until the second month in order to allow time for the necessary preparations. Its proper celebration took precedence over the traditional date (30:2). Similarly, in the exigencies of the time, the importance of sharing in the festival was deemed to override some of the usual ritual requirements (30:18–20), something perhaps for us to reflect on in determining our priorities in difficult situations. This was not done lightly. Hezekiah prayed for the people and the Lord heard. He is, as 30:9 says, gracious and merciful (*hannun werahum*). Strict attention to the externals of worship had never been sufficient. Heart commitment was what mattered, the prophets said. Hezekiah had understood.

3 Practical action, faith, prayer

2 Chronicles 32:1–20, 24–26

The Chronicler seems sometimes to have an over-simplistic, almost mechanical view of reward and punishment. This is an interesting exception. Enemy attack is not interpreted here as punishment for wrongdoing. The writer himself finds it noteworthy that 'after all that Hezekiah had so faithfully done, Sennacherib king of Assyria came and invaded Judah' (v. 1, NIV). The year was 701BC. Sennacherib, a powerful ruler, was bent on empire, and we have (now in the British Museum) Sennacherib's own triumphant account of his conquests, how '[Hezekiah] himself I shut up like a caged bird, within Jerusalem, his royal city'. This dire situation is reflected possibly in Isaiah 1:8, where Zion is described as standing solitary in its desolate land 'like a shelter in a cucumber field, like a besieged city'. Notice the blend of faith and practical action on Hezekiah's part (vv. 1–8). The enemy's propaganda is interesting: Hezekiah must without doubt have offended his God by removing all his shrines and altars save one (v. 12).

A point of special archeological interest is 'Hezekiah's tunnel' in Jerusalem (v. 30), rediscovered in 1880. It is eerie to walk through it, lit only by flickering candles. A fascinating inscription, now in the Museum of the Ancient Orient at Istanbul, records the moment when the miners, tunnelling from two ends, finally broke through the rock and heard each other's voices. (It is fair to add that some scholars have argued against identifying this tunnel with Hezekiah's work, although not entirely convincingly.)

As often in Chronicles, the writer emphasizes the important role of prophets. Here it is Isaiah giving support to Hezekiah in urgent prayer. It is worth contrasting Hezekiah's anxious prayer in 2 Kings 19:15–19 with the total confidence in God expressed here in Chronicles (vv. 7–8). But the Chronicler is realistic. No one is perfect, and sadly Hezekiah's story is marred by one blemish at the end of his life. He, too, became proud and unresponsive to the Lord's goodness (v. 25). For details of his illness, see 2 Kings 20 and Isaiah 38. The Chronicler's message for his contemporaries is clear: trust the Lord and stay faithful to him.

4 Manasseh: a king reformed

2 Chronicles 33:1–20

From the high point of Hezekiah's reforms and heartfelt commitment to the Lord, the narrative sinks to a new low with Manasseh, his son and successor who became king at the age of twelve. Other young kings before him, Joash aged seven (24:1) and Uzziah at sixteen (26:1), had wise counsellors to guide them. Not so Manasseh. Hezekiah's reforms were reversed. With the distasteful treatment of his son (v. 6), we are back in the days of his grandfather Ahaz. Altars to other gods and a carved idol were introduced even into the temple—a deliberate, arrogant offence perpetrated against the holy place and against the Lord.

As so often, like king, like people: they were led astray. Verse 9 describes the depth to which they sank. The reference to Manasseh's exile (v. 11) has given rise to much debate among commentators. Has it a historical basis? There is no reference to it in 2 Kings 21 or in any of the Assyrian records known to us. Yet it is unlikely to have been an invention of the Chronicler, who sees in it a turning point in Manasseh's life. It has become clear elsewhere that the Chronicler drew not only on the earlier tradition of Kings but on independent sources.

This is a most remarkable chapter. From the depths of degradation, of deliberate offence against the sanctity of the temple, and even from exile, there was the possibility of repentance and restoration for Manasseh—and if for him, why not for others? What a word of hope for the Chronicler's diminished community! They too had benefited from restoration, the return from exile under Cyrus the Persian. They were back home in Judah with their temple restored and its worship once again at the community's heart. Always before them, however, lay the choice of two ways—of trust in the Lord or of the downward spiral into despair and loss of identity. Manasseh's repentance was expressed in action (vv. 14–16), always the fruit of true repentance

This remarkable chapter offers two main lessons for us, as for the Chronicler's first readers. (1) Every leader is responsible for his or her own actions. The past can either be built on or its warnings ignored. (2) However low the depths to which leader and people have sunk, the situation can, in the Lord's mercy, be redeemed. With God a fresh start is always available.

5 Finding the book of the law

2 Chronicles 34:1–18, 22–28

Josiah, like his great-grandfather Hezekiah, was one of the outstanding kings in Judah's history. Coming young to the throne, he began his restoration of the temple when only 20 years old. It was a pivotal moment for the nation. During the work on the temple, the law scroll (generally thought to be part of Deuteronomy) was found. Its content caused consternation.

The fact that they chose to consult Huldah—a prophetess, obviously highly respected—is interesting, for this was the time of Jeremiah's ministry. Sadly, Huldah fades from view thereafter, back into the shadows where women in the Old Testament are usually to be found, unlike Jeremiah, of whom we read much in the book of that name. It is a salutary reminder, however, that there were women who played a key role in Israel's history despite their muted part in the narrative (see, among others, especially Exodus 1:17; 2:10).

With the waning of Assyrian influence at this time, Josiah's reforms extended even into the northern kingdom (vv. 6–7). It is likely that he had hopes of reuniting north and south as in the days of past glory.

Although, for reasons of brevity, chapter 35 is not included in our reading, a brief comparison of this chapter with 2 Kings 22 and 23 illustrates the chronicler's independent perspective. The reinstating of the Passover, mentioned briefly in 2 Kings 23:21–23, is greatly expanded in Chronicles 35 in line with the writer's interest in all things liturgical, influenced in its detail probably by the practice of his own time. Another striking difference is the explanation for Josiah's untimely death, explained in 2 Kings 23:26–27 as judgment on the wrong done by Manasseh, his predecessor. Chronicles gives its own different explanation in 35:22, although how Josiah was expected to discern that the words of the Egyptian Neco were 'from the mouth of the Lord' is a mystery.

The history of this period (609BC; 35:20ff) is clarified for us by the clay tablets of the Babylonian Chronicle, a reliable, probably contemporary record of each year's main events. Neco moved to support the waning Assyrian power against the rising Babylonians. Josiah's ill-advised intervention against Neco led to his untimely end. His tragic death resembles that of Ahab. Despite disguise, disaster strikes (35:22). It is of interest that the Chronicler includes the unfulfilled prophecy of a peaceful end, in 34:28.

6 Judah's last sad days

The action speeds up, as if the Chronicler wants to hurry over the last sad chapter. Four kings in quick succession within 23 years bring Judah's story up to the exile. The succession passed first to Josiah's eldest son, Jehoahaz. But Judah was weak and Egypt strong, and Jehoiakim, his brother, soon displaced him, to become notorious for his high-handed hostility to the prophet Jeremiah. A dramatic confrontation between king and prophet is recounted in Jeremiah 36, with the king defiantly burning the prophet's scroll column by column (36:23). Jeremiah had performed symbolic actions, acted parables signifying the certainty of the Lord's word. The king's act may be intended as a symbolic action designed to invalidate Jeremiah's prophecies of doom. The brief reign of his young son Jehoiachin ('eight years', v. 9, is probably a scribal error for 18, as in 2 Kings 24:8) ended in exile in Babylon, the ascendant power since Assyria's fall in 612BC.

The end for Judah was brutal. Zedekiak, another of Josiah's sons, resolutely refused to heed Jeremiah's warnings and rebelled against Nebuchadnezzar. Wholesale slaughter of young and old followed, as well as destruction of the temple and city (587BC). Earlier in the book, the building of the temple was described at length. Now its destruction requires few words—the final curtain, it must have seemed, on a tragic story of persistent unfaithfulness to the Lord and the failure of faith in the reliability of his word. Far from it! Jeremiah's dire warnings were fulfilled but in the darkest times with God there is hope. The exile was not proof of his weakness but of his strength, and he too could save, for had not Jeremiah also prophesied a future?

Cyrus the Persian was to be God's instrument (v. 22). The closing words, identical to the beginning of Ezra, are a remarkably upbeat ending to a story in which, despite intermittent brighter periods, the darkness seems to close in even faster at the end. In the distinctive arrangement of the Hebrew Bible, this expression of hope is the last word. The Lord is never defeated. The Chronicler's own community owed its existence to the eventual return from exile under Cyrus. Truly a dramatic ending to the book!

Guidelines

The Chronicler's story comes to a sad end. After the seesawing of history with its new beginnings and lost opportunities, the land is desolate, the temple plundered, burned and destroyed, the people slaughtered or in exile. Where is hope now?

As in Ahaz's story (28:24), with the temple shut down and Baal altars everywhere, this was not the final blow. God is the great reverser of desperate situations. What he asks of his people, of us, is deep commitment, renewed trust and a readiness to do his will. However dark the situation, however hopeless the apathy and indifference, slowly and silently his kingdom grows, as in Jesus' parable of the yeast and the dough (Matthew 13:33). The words of 36:16 are chilling: 'mocking... despising... scoffing... until the wrath of the Lord against his people became so great that there was no remedy.' Yet here is the wonder of the gospel. The Lord took on himself the humiliation and scoffing and by his death brought life.

We have read the ancient stories and seen them interpreted by the Chronicler for his contemporaries in a changed world. The word, God's word, is living and active. Down through the centuries it reaches us in a world of yet greater change. What demands does it make on us? What heart-searching? And what encouragement for our days of the 'church in exile'?

The visionary word comes with reassurance over the centuries: 'He who sat upon the throne said, "Behold, I make all things new"' (Revelation 21:5, RSV).

FURTHER READING

Gwilym H. Jones, *1 & 2 Chronicles* (Old Testament Guides), Sheffield Academic Press, 1993.

H.G.M. Williamson, *1 and 2 Chronicles* (New Century Bible Commentary), Eerdmans/Marshall, Morgan & Scott, 1982.

R.J. Coggins, *The First and Second Books of the Chronicles* (Cambridge Bible Commentary on the New English Bible), Cambridge University Press, 1976.

COLOSSIANS

'Ancient texts were not always ancient... Paul's letter to the Christian community in Colossae was once a piece of contemporary correspondence to a particular community in a particular place and time. And like our time, theirs was a time of empire.' (*Colossians Remixed*, p. 38)

This reminder in a recent book on Colossians is well worth taking seriously. Paul's letter to the Colossians was a genuine letter, written in a particular context. The precise date and place of writing do not matter greatly (generally thought to be about AD60, from Rome): what is clear is that it was written to a Christian community in Colossae, a city in modern-day Turkey, then firmly within the Roman empire. Paul had never been there (see the notes on 1:1–12), yet he felt connected to these people and wrote them this letter, which is warm and encouraging while also being theologically profound. It is not taken up with endless problem solving (as we find in the Corinthian correspondence), nor is it occasioned by a crisis (as in, say, Galatians). Rather, Paul addresses fundamental issues of the supremacy, sufficiency and accessibility of Christ. He does this in a context where Lordship would be seen as a challenge to Rome, and accessibility and sufficiency as a challenge to 'advanced' religious or moral teaching and esoteric or 'worthy' practices.

The Colossians' context was different from our own, yet there are many similarities. Our culture proclaims that its 'way of life' brings freedom and prosperity, just as the Roman empire did, and that it is the only rational option. Religion is allowed as long as it takes its place within this 'way of life' rather than challenging it and suggesting that there is a better alternative. Our culture is also full of claims of new products, self-help guides and lifestyle regimes which will help us to better ourselves and achieve happiness (and be 'one step ahead of the game').

Colossians has many similarities to Ephesians, though at times Ephesians seems more 'universalized'—not so much focused on a particular community. Colossians is also close to Philemon and Philippians, many scholars seeing them as also being written from the same place (by Paul in prison) at a similar time.

1 Growing and bearing fruit

Colossians 1:1–12

Paul's warmth towards the Colossians is almost overpowering; verses 3–12 form just three sentences in the Greek, phrases tumbling over each other in Paul's joyous description of the 'holy and faithful brothers and sisters in Christ at Colossae'. While Paul generally starts his letters with thanksgiving (an interesting principle), here it is particularly pronounced. This is probably because the Colossian church is genuinely doing well: the rest of the letter seems more to warn of potential problems than highlight actual ones. It may also connect with the fact that this is one of only two letters (Romans being the other) that Paul wrote to congregations he had not visited (2:1; hinted at in this passage). Paul is overjoyed because the Colossian church is proof that his mission is succeeding, for any transmission of the faith can be judged a success when the recipients can successfully pass it on themselves. The aim is not another disciple but a disciple who can make other disciples; not a church but a church that can plant other churches. Paul based himself in Ephesus for a few years (Acts 19:1–20) but now the church has spread to surrounding cities such as Colossae (and Laodicea and Hierapolis, 4:13). Truly the gospel is bearing fruit 'all over the world' (v. 6).

Paul parallels this spread of the gospel with the development of the spiritual and moral life of those who receive it (vv. 9–10). In both cases the image of growth and bearing fruit is used. The growth of the number of believers goes hand in hand with the increased fruitfulness of their lives. Sometimes, in our churches, we play one of these developments off against the other, justifying a lack of growth in numbers by suggesting that our church is growing in depth instead, as if they were alternatives. Both, however, Paul teaches, are part of the same fruitful growth.

Throughout this passage we encounter key ideas in Paul's thought: 'holy and faithful', 'love and hope', 'enduring with patience', 'joy' and 'sharing the inheritance'. Striking, though, in verses 9–10 is the double mention of knowledge of God (or of his will) together with spiritual wisdom and understanding. Throughout the letter, the importance of truly understanding what God has achieved in Jesus continues to be unpacked.

2 Christ is everything

The previous section finished with mention of God's strength and the inheritance awaiting the Colossians, but also of the need to endure. This points to the underlying tension in Paul's message. He proclaims, and they have believed, in Jesus Christ as Lord, but they live in a world in which there are other lords. In particular, they live in the middle of the Roman empire, whose military power was unrivalled and which proclaimed that it brought peace and fruitfulness. Its supremacy in every area of life was proclaimed in the great buildings of the city, the coinage used, the festivals and in the impossibility of even contemplating rebellion. Against this, what is Christ?

Christ is everything. He is the face and presence of God (vv. 15, 19), the designer, purpose and sustainer of all creation (vv. 16, 17), the source of new life and true peace (vv. 18, 20, 21). Compared to him, the emperor and all the glory, boasts and achievements of the empire are nothing. God has transferred the believers from the 'kingdom of darkness' to that of his Son (v. 13). Paul may not be using the phrase 'kingdom of darkness' merely as a synonym for the 'empire of Rome', for his Jewish history would have taught him that empires come and go. Nevertheless, any talk of 'another kingdom' would have been treason, a challenge to the empire's supremacy. If the believers have been transferred into the kingdom of the Lord of creation, the face and presence of God, then they are clearly no longer loyal subjects of the empire of Rome.

We easily fall into behaving as if Christ claims Lordship of only part of our lives—the religious dimension as opposed to our work, our money, our lifestyle, our politics. But if this vision of Christ is true, then Christ claims Lordship of everything—Monday as well as Sunday, the private and the public, the 'sacred' and the 'secular'. The challenge is not so much to agree that this is true, but to recognize what, in our lives, challenges Christ's Lordship.

3 The mystery

'What's really going on?' is a perennial human question. In our age, there is no shortage of people offering to let us in on 'the secret', which makes sense of all that we see around us. Some suggest that the secret is determinism (choice is but an illusion), others that 'choice' itself is the secret (our humanity is expressed through making choices), or perhaps all that we see is actually part of a shadowy CIA plot or the construction of 'the media'.

The secret is out, says Paul. The word used can be translated 'secret' or 'mystery', the background being Jewish prophecy and apocalyptic, in which God's plan is kept secret in heaven and is unknowable—mysterious —for humans. Just the fact that the secret 'hidden throughout the ages' (1:26) is now revealed to those such as the Colossians is itself startling. It is not the wise or powerful in their day who know 'what is really going on' but it is them—ordinary women and men. They know because they are 'the saints'—the 'holy ones', made holy by Christ's death (1:22).

The secret is Christ himself (2:2) or, more particularly, 'Christ in you [even Gentiles], the hope of glory' (1:27). The incarnation, the invisible God being perfectly revealed and embodied in the man Jesus (1:15, 19), is indeed unexpected. This has good claim to be the unique feature of Christianity compared to all other religions, that one particular man gave us the perfect representation (the word 'image' would be used of a reflection in a mirror) of God, and indeed was the embodiment of God. Jesus did not just teach about God or speak for God, but in meeting him people were meeting God. If that is troubling to many, then the idea of this Christ being 'in you' is the final straw. Christ, the creator and sustainer of everything, the embodiment of God, is 'in' them.

The impact of this knowledge, for Paul, is twofold. First, he works to make this mystery known (1:25); this secret and hope of the ages is for everyone (note 'everyone' occurring three times in verse 28). Second, if we have 'all the riches of assured understanding' (2:2) then we cannot be deceived by plausible-sounding arguments (v. 4): all we need to do is to continue in Christ (v. 6). But are we too cynical in our politically correct age to believe that we have the secret of the ages?

4 Religious practices

Colossians 2:8–23

'See to it that no one takes you captive' (v. 8). In this section of the letter, Paul hints at the concerns he has. The idea that there was a full-blown

'Colossian heresy' seems to be the result of thinking that every Pauline letter must be responding to a particular problem. The general nature of this passage suggests rather that these are concerns that Paul has for believers like the Colossians, not that he has heard particular reports about them.

Paul's concerns revolve around 'religious practices'—particular food and drink, holy days, angels (vv. 16–18), instructions as to what one can or cannot do (v. 21). His answer is straightforward: there is no need to follow any such practices; they have no value. Such practices, though, have the appearance of piety and thus can give the impression that those who do not follow them are, in some way, second class. Do not believe it, Paul says. Such practices are 'empty deceit' (v. 8); 'do not let anyone condemn you' over them (v. 16); 'do not let anyone disqualify you' over them (v. 18).

Why are 'religious practices' empty and meaningless? Paul's final reason is that they don't work (v. 23). Even if they appear to be aimed at good results (wisdom, piety, humility), they don't deliver. And the reason they don't deliver is that they are merely human traditions (vv. 8, 18, 22), not based on actual knowledge of God, which is available in Christ.

There is more, though. Such religious practices are seen as the sphere of the 'elemental spirits of the universe' (v. 20). This ambiguous phrase could mean 'the way the world is' or 'controlling spiritual beings', though Paul and his readers would probably have seen these meanings as linked. The demand to follow religious practices is in fact a demand to submit to these 'spirits', to conform to ideas of what 'being religious' means. In response, Paul returns to the theme of chapter 1. Christ defines what 'being religious' truly means, for the whole fullness of God dwells bodily in him' (v. 9). In him they have fullness (v. 10), have been released from 'flesh' and 'the world' (vv. 11, 20), have died and been made alive (vv. 12, 13), and have the substance not the shadow (v. 17). Christ is the ruler of all things (v. 10) and has broken the hold of the 'elemental spirits' on the cross (vv. 13–15).

We see here a message that runs throughout Paul's letters. There is a real danger in accepting as necessary or even desirable anything that is not Christ. What begins as an 'optional extra' ends up undermining Christ's Lordship and making others, or even ourselves, wonder if there is some 'secret knowledge' that needs to be added to the basic message of Christ in us. On the contrary, we just need to hold on to him (1:23; 2:6–7, 19). The question for us is obvious: what religious practices do we value or rely on?

5 New life

'So…' Paul writes (v. 1). Colossians and Romans (12:1) are both marked by this very clear move from statements of what is true (recapped in 3:1–4) to advice and instruction as to how to live (the rest of the chapter).

It is worth considering this logic, that truths about our own union with Christ in his death and resurrection (the language looks back to 2:11–13) transform our way of life; that we are called to 'be who we are', to live out what has happened to us. This exposes a particular approach to ethics, in which ethics becomes a matter of character rather than of 'codes of conduct'. When Paul urges that the believers lead 'lives worthy of the Lord' (1:10), the meaning is not 'lives that God's rules judge to be worthwhile' but 'lives that reflect the fact that Christ is in us'. We are not being urged to live more moral lives, certainly not to follow more moral practices (which would lead us into the dangers explored in the previous chapter), but simply to live lives that more truly reflect what we now are. We might even say that there is no such thing as 'Christian ethics' but only 'Christian character'.

The difference is subtle but suggestive, for it implies that no one can teach what Christians ought to do (indeed, 'ought' plunges us back into the regulations of chapter 2), but rather that we should focus on who we truly are (as a result of Christ's work), urge that that identity is lived out in practice, and let the conduct follow. Nevertheless, people want examples, so Paul unpacks what appropriate behaviour would look like; the danger is that these examples become a new set of 'oughts'.

This logic also raises questions about 'Christian ethics' as a basis for morality for those who do not believe, for if the 'be' is not connected to 'what you are', then is it not just another set of regulations? Yet surely the lifestyle outlined in the rest of the chapter would be good for all?

The outlines for living (vv. 5–17) are worth meditating upon. They depict what we should be—or, rather, are—truly like, and provide a destination towards which we can resolve to travel. What step can we take today?

6 New family

It is sometimes said that Christians live in the 'now and not yet'—the tension between the world as it is and the world as it should and one day will be. In the language of Colossians 1:13, we may have been transferred into the kingdom of his beloved Son, but we still have to endure life in the Roman empire, or whatever our equivalent may be.

Jesus taught that those who followed God's will were his true family (Mark 3:31–35), and Paul talks of the 'family of faith' (Galatians 6:10). Chapter 4 expresses this idea. Paul depicts a wide circle of 'fellow workers', some of whom the Colossians probably knew, others they may not have done. But they are not alone. They may feel like an embattled tiny minority loyal to an empire other than Rome's, but they are part of this wide family. In our communication age, we are better informed about fellow Christians in other churches, cities and countries than our ancestors ever were, yet this doesn't seem to translate into a belief that they are part of our family. We, like the Colossians, can benefit from this wider vision.

Within all this, however, there are the existing families. Whatever else is said, the Colossians belong to households of husbands and wives, slaves and masters, children and parents, and these relationships bring with them expectations of what being a wife, husband, master, slave, parent or child 'means'—how one ought to behave. What did their death and resurrection 'in Christ' mean for these relationships? What do they mean for ours?

Paul's approach is, effectively, that the structures of society are as they are. He does not call on the Colossians to change them (how could they?) but rather gives pointers on how someone who has shared Christ's death and resurrection might live within these structures and expectations. The key point appears to be about living these relationships in the light of Christ's Lordship. Therefore, those who have power (husbands, parents, masters) should live mindful of the fact that God also has power over them (explicit in 4:1). Those without power (wives, children, slaves) can see their position transformed by living out their humble state not as a dictate of the world, but as a service of Christ (again, explicit in 3:22–25). Notice the explicit mention of 'the Lord' in the case of the three 'weaker' partners.

Such teaching can seem problematic to us, partly because we feel that Paul ought to have urged his contemporaries to overturn the structures of their society. We also interpret the teaching as 'how the structures *should be*', not as 'how to live given what the structures *were*' (although those who follow this interpretation in respect of wives and children seem rarely to do so in respect of slavery). We could conclude that Paul was more realistic than we prefer our religious teachers to be. He gave advice that could be followed; strangely, it can be convenient if teaching remains merely aspirational, for then we have a ready excuse to ignore it in practice. Can we see past the theoretical arguments and decide how the fact that Christ is in us should transform our most important relationships today?

Guidelines

Colossians is a rich text, full of powerful ideas. I would suggest three of those ideas for further contemplation: the supremacy of Christ, the sufficiency of Christ, and living lives worthy of the Lord. Think again about these ideas, and ask God to show you how each one could shape your life.

- Christ is supreme, above all things. *Everything* you can imagine is part of what was created through him and for him and is sustained by him. What aspects of your life, or your concerns for others or situations in the world, need to be put in perspective by the supremacy of Christ?
- Christ is sufficient. Nothing else is needed; there are no more secrets. This is a powerful message, which we might expect to be welcomed, but humans seem incapable of believing that something so important can be simple, and so we create more 'baggage' to surround it. You may believe that Christ is sufficient, but your actions may suggest that there are practices or ideas which, deep down, you think are at least half necessary. Perhaps God can reveal them to you.
- Rather than trying to follow the rules, we should be aiming to 'live lives worthy of the Lord' or to 'be who we are'. The idea of rules to be kept comes easily to us, but the idea that we are called simply to live out our true nature is far more disturbing and powerful. We don't know what effect this letter had on the Colossians; what matters now is what effect we will allow it to have on us.

FURTHER READING

Brian Walsh and Sylvia Keesmaat, *Colossians Remixed*, Paternoster, 2004.

Tom Wright, *Paul for Everyone: The Prison Letters*, SPCK, 2002.

Peter O'Brien, *Colossians—Philemon*, Word, 1982.

James Dunn, *The Epistles to the Colossians and to Philemon*, Eerdmans, 1996.

JUDGES 1—8

The book of Judges is not about judges as we understand them, but about the leaders of Israel. The judges were tribal leaders who arose in a time of need and, despite occasionally having judicial functions, were first and foremost the civic leaders. In biblical history, the period of the Judges is a time of reflection and experimentation. Having recently entered the promised land, Israel needs to organize and establish its position, and the people show normal human failings. It is a period of instability that will be resolved only with the establishment of the Israelite monarchy in the time of David.

The book contains many examples of failure, violence and missed opportunities. It is thus a reflection of everyday life and, probably more than in any other biblical book, we are faced with a troubled and bloody history. The writers have not been afraid to describe the reality of life, and they have incorporated these descriptions into national tales that must have been repeated and remembered through the years. The beliefs and national identity of Israel are built upon these tales, and it is a remarkable fact that the religion has arisen not from philosophical reflection but from remembrance and recounting of their history. Encounter with the hardships and failures of daily life, and eventually the overcoming of them, are the basis for a secure faith in God.

In our readings over the next two weeks, examples will be seen of anger, greed, unjust vengeance, indecisiveness and moral ambiguity. These human traits are representative of the search for God and the wrong turnings on the road of enquiry. The very opening of the book is a question to God, a reminder of the dependence of the people upon him, but also of their failure to listen properly. All humanity is at fault.

1 Victories against the Canaanites

Judges 1:1–13

The opening of the book is both confusing and fast-paced. The feeling of uncertainty among the people and the desperate situation in which they find themselves are expressed by this unsettling account. The reason for the instability is the loss of their leader (v. 1) and the failure to complete the conquest of the land, as can be seen by the end of chapter 1. Verse 1 speaks of the death of Joshua, although his death is not recorded until chapter 2, and some translations prefer to read Moses (as in Joshua 1:1). The people of Israel have gathered together (probably at Gilgal: see 2:1) to enquire of the Lord, in a religious ceremony, which of the twelve tribes should lead the united tribal forces against the Canaanite tribes. God chooses Judah and gives the land to him, although first he must remove the inhabitants. He therefore achieves victory over the Canaanites and Perizzites (vv. 4–5), the rulers of Jerusalem (v. 8), Hebron (v. 10) and Debir (vv. 11–13) and, later in our story, the rulers of Zephath (v. 17). The fast succession of victories suggests the pace of the army as it makes inroads into the country.

The humiliation of Adoni-Bezek by the removal of his thumbs and toes, though gruesome to us, was a common type of punishment for defeated enemies. It is representative of his loss of power and perhaps, too, his ability to sacrifice as a priest-king. His expression regarding the 70 kings is a reference to the subjugation of all the kings (70 as a perfect or complete number) whom he had defeated, and recognition that he was symbolically receiving the treatment he had meted out to others. The victory of Adoni-Bezek is, therefore, indicative of a victory in the region for Judah, conquering the supreme Canaanite king. The names of some of the cities are important for the later history of Israel, and no doubt are mentioned here to indicate that they have been cleared of Canaanite pollution from idol worship before reappearing later in Israel's history. Jerusalem was to become the centre of temple worship, and Hebron was to become the site of David's coronation and possibly palace (2 Samuel 5:3).

For us, the tales of killing and war under the guidance of God are difficult to understand. Here it should be clear that the purpose is to remove the tyrants controlling the region, and especially the arch-tyrant Adoni-Bezek and those who controlled Jerusalem and Hebron. It is a hard choice to take, and the people call upon God to ask who should be the leader. Under sound leadership the best action ought to be taken for the sake of removing evil but also preserving life.

2 Recognition of failings

Judges 2:1–15

After the initial victories have turned into defeats at the end of chapter 1, a message from God explains the failures. An angel of God reminds Israel of its history, of God's loyalty and promise, and how the people have disobeyed him. This accounts for the continued resistance that Israel is facing in driving out the other nations. The first response from the people of Israel is to weep in recognition of their faults, foreshadowing the weeping of the people again at the end of the book (21:2). Despite the reminder of God's promise, nothing changes from the beginning to the end of the book: Israel fails and must wait for a king to establish peace in 1 Samuel. The weeping is so significant that the place is actually named Bochim, which in Hebrew means 'weeping' (v. 5).

The brief passage that follows (vv. 6–7) implies that some stability ensued once Israel had recognized their guilt, although soon afterwards Joshua died. His death is also recounted in Joshua 24 and, as for all the great figures in the history, his burial is given some prominence. Here it helps to define the land, that his bones are placed in the land of his inheritance. In contrast to Moses, Joshua was able to enter the promised land, and the territory of Ephraim in the north is marked as part of Israel's possession through his burial in that place.

With the loss of their leader Joshua, the Israelites once more fall into disobedience. They are attracted by the gods of their neighbours and their disloyalty to the God of Israel is patent. They are accused of following after Baal, the supreme god of the Canaanite pantheon. They also worship the Ashteroth, which were cult statues, perhaps representing a female consort of Baal, and thus break the first two of the Ten Commandments. The consequences are dire for Israel and they are unable to gain victory in their conflicts with the neighbouring tribes.

3 The judges arise

Judges 2:16–23

A solution is offered Israel for their troubles, but they do not take it. Here we have the first mention of the judges after whom the book is named, although they are not as yet given any special role. At this point, too, the judges are not named, but are merely described as a body. In the rest of the book we will meet individuals who are judges with personal characteristics and have varying degrees of success. Each time the Lord raises up judges, the people do not listen to them and 'prostitute' after other gods (v. 17), a strong metaphor for disobedience.

This passage expresses succinctly the cyclical nature of the book: every time God raises up judges, the people go astray and God must raise up more judges. It serves as a summary of the whole theme of the book and prepares the reader for the tales of individual judges. This cycle of salvation and falling away from God will not be resolved by the end of the book, and must await the rising up of Kings David and Solomon.

The troubles that Israel fall into are said to be a divine test (v. 22) for the people. The biblical idea of testing is exemplified by the most famous and disturbing of tests, when Abraham was asked to sacrifice his only son, Isaac (Genesis 22). Abraham's loyalty to and fear of God were proven through the test, and in Judges God is testing Israel since they are unable to follow his laws by obeying his judges. From our perspective, God's testing of the people by putting before them conquering enemies seems a harsh decision. The disloyalty of Israel requires it, though. Even if God provides such difficult testing, it is balanced by the help he does provide when we are loyal to him, just as he repeatedly raised up faithful judges. God's ways are not always easy or clear to us, but we can trust that he will always provide for those who trust in him.

4 The victory of Ehud

Judges 3:12–30

One of the first successful leaders is Ehud, although he is called a deliverer rather than a judge (v. 15). His victory combines humour with a humiliating death for the enemy king, Eglon. It is recounted like a folktale, a story that could be repeated to pass on to later generations the history of Israel. History does not always have to be tales of great political achievements, and here the account establishes a national saga in people's minds through memorable tales.

The memorable elements of the story are brought about by humorous wordplays and precise details that contribute to the storytelling effect of the tale. Ehud is described as left-handed (v. 15), a detail that does not seem to be important for the story, except that it allows him to remove the dagger easily from beside his right thigh (v. 21). However, his being left-handed is mentioned in the same verse as his tribal designation, Benjamin-ite, which in Hebrew means 'right-handed'. The author is obviously having fun with the wordplay. The same can be said of the detailed account of the death of Eglon. The dagger is thrust into his belly until the hilt is enclosed by the fat. It is a lurid description, but again made more memorable by the similar sound of the words for 'dagger' (*hereb*) and 'fat' (*heleb*) in Hebrew.

This is a curious story of trickery over an enemy king that leads to victory over Moab and peace for 80 years (v. 30). It is one of many personalized stories in Judges, in which greater focus is given to the defeat and death of a leader than to accounts of battles. It allows for contrast between the successful judges of Israel and the failing leaders of other nations. In this case, Eglon is presented in humiliating terms as a very fat man, so much so that Ehud cannot withdraw his dagger when it is enveloped in the fat. Eglon also seems to be relaxing in a cooling summer chamber, with the implication that he is luxuriating when he should be governing. His servants think, when he does not appear, that he must be relieving himself (v. 24)—an unflattering image, but with the irony that dirt had in fact been excreted from his body, only by a different means (v. 22). In contrast, we hear little of the personal details of Ehud, who appears only in this brief passage and then lives victorious after defeating such a comical figure.

We see in this passage a fine example of memorable storytelling. National history is built upon stories that can be repeated and, although the story might seem comical and even crude, it is the ability to capture the audience's attention that is most important. The people of Israel could remember these tales and reinforce their self-identity through recalling such acts of their nation's history.

5 The hand of a woman

Judges 4:1–9

Despite the period of peace ushered in by Ehud, Israel once more finds itself in trouble. The solution is unexpected but important for Israel's own understanding of its history. Deborah, a woman and the only female judge in the book, is introduced in brief but striking terms. Although she is identified by her relationship to her husband ('wife of Lappidoth', v. 4), as would be normal for a woman, this is not the first piece of information we learn. She is first of all a prophetess—a rare office at the time—then wife and then judge. She is independent and endowed with many skills. Indeed, since the husband's name is unknown elsewhere, some scholars believe that the phrase 'wife of Lappidoth' should be read as 'a fiery woman'. She would then be a woman of a fiery personality, which is brought out by her behaviour later in the chapter, and this emphasis on a character trait would be in keeping with other descriptions of judges, such as Ehud with his left-handedness.

Deborah's role up to this point has been as an adjudicator of cases, while sitting under the tree. In the rest of the Bible, only Moses shares this role with her (Exodus 18:13). The region of Bethel was an important site for communicating with God and was the location of Jacob's vision of heaven (Genesis 28), but from such a peaceful scene Deborah will be chosen to lead Israel in military affairs. She vows that she will lead Israel to victory against the enemy general Sisera, enforcing surprise with the words 'the hand of a woman' (v. 9). The same phrase is picked up in the tale of Judith in the Apocrypha, a much later account of a similar victory by a woman.

There are far fewer biblical examples of leadership roles for women than for men, but examples such as Deborah remind us that, at the time, women did have a greater role in society than we might expect. It is noticeable that Deborah is not introduced with any great emphasis on her gender. Her role as prophetess and judge are noted without great comment, since it seems to have been an accepted convention. It is only when she crosses the line and becomes involved in military affairs that the author underlines the fact that her exploits are 'by the hand of a woman'. Female leaders are considered so routine that it is not worthy of comment for the writer.

6 Hospitality subverted

While the men are indecisive in the face of the Canaanite army, Deborah resolves to take matters into her own hands. Although she is assisted by Barak, commander of the Israelite forces, it is clear from the outset that Deborah is in charge, and she gives the orders to Barak (v. 14). Once more, the main battle scene is brief (vv. 15–16), since the focus is on individuals, their characters and their achievements. Deborah had predicted victory by the hand of a woman, and accordingly we are now introduced to Jael, wife of Heber, who tricks Sisera. Little is said about who Jael is, allowing attention to be placed on her actions, brutal and successful that they are.

Precisely how Jael was allowed access to Sisera's tent is unclear. Once she was there, she was more than hospitable, but her hospitality was to be broken by her final action. She first covers him with a blanket so that he can rest. Sisera, naturally thirsty from the battle, asks for water, and Jael is more than generous by giving him milk. Milk, however, has the effect of inducing sleep, and Jael continues serving him by ensuring that no one should disturb his sleep. Nevertheless, all these acts of hospitality provide her with the opportunity to drive a tent peg through his head, and thereby she subverts her generosity. The ineffectiveness of men is underlined first by Sisera's inability to move through weariness (v. 21) and then by the summoning of Barak to see what has been done (v. 22).

The story of Jael's defeat of Sisera strikes us as disturbing in a number of respects. The gruesome nature of the death, the abuse of the laws of hospitality, the trickery required for the victory and the savagery of the woman are not glorious exploits for a national saga. The fact that the section ends with the statement that God gave victory (v. 23) hardly satisfies this unease. It is, however, a memorable tale and the purpose in recording it was to provide a story that could be recalled from generation to generation, evoking delight and shock at the same time. Its ultimate message is one of failure. The men are ineffective on the part of both the Canaanite and the Israelite armies. Disloyalty and disorder have reached such an extreme that only the women can find a solution. Sadly, that solution is horrific but necessary.

Guidelines

From the opening of the book of Judges, we are presented with a question: how does one choose leaders? Israel asks the question of God, and the answer that he gives—the provision of judges—is only temporary, owing to Israel's own failings. In today's world, the issue of good and faithful leaders is constantly before us. We are ready to criticize the wrongs committed by them and to look for ethical alternatives. Certainly it is right to choose leaders who are seeking to apply ethical values and implement policies for the greater good. However, the book of Judges reminds us how difficult it is to be a leader. The realities of life and the frailties of humans make it ever more difficult to make the right decisions in government. Currently, world leaders are tackling global problems for which there are no easy solutions and, if they make mistakes in the face of such difficulties, it is only natural. Israel at the time of the judges was also facing grave dangers and made mistakes in the course of its attempts to resolve the situation. We should understand our leaders as well as criticize them.

The book of Judges also reminds us of our own individual responsibilities within the world. Despite the selection of good leaders, and even with the support of God, the nation was not successful, since it was the people's choice not to listen and to go after other gods. The refrain is repeated throughout the book that the children of Israel did evil or did not remember their God. Without cooperation and involvement from the people, governments cannot be sustained. Our duty goes beyond that of voting and choosing our leaders, since it is our task to engage in our local communities and develop the practice needed for healing the wounds of the world. With the current global crises facing us, it can be easy to feel helpless, as Israel did before its enemies, but if each of us works towards greater understanding, it can be a contribution towards the global peace that we all seek.

1 Song of Deborah

Judges 5:1–31

One of the great poems of the Bible is the victory song by Deborah, one of a number of songs of joy sung by women, comparable to Mary's song of praise in Luke's Gospel (1:46–55). The language is complex but we can enjoy its poetic nature without worrying about every detail. The first half of the poem recounts the military victories, expressed in terms of God's power over creation. It is striking here that Deborah is called a mother in Israel (v. 7), suggesting that her role is the most important for the safety and future of Israel. Likewise, Jael is said to be blessed above all women (v. 24) for her killing of Sisera (vv. 25–27).

The greatest difference in the poem's account of the victory compared to the previous account in chapter 4 is the introduction of Sisera's mother, who, with great pathos, awaits the return of her son (vv. 28–30). It looks forward to a more successful mother-and-son relationship in the story of Samson (Judges 13—14). It also adds to the irony of the whole account, reinforcing the superior role of women to men, since she is surrounded by wise ladies (v. 29), and providing a contrast between Sisera's mother and Deborah as mother of Israel. The irony continues when the mother hears the sound of chariots, expecting it as a sign of her son's return. It is those powerful chariots that should have granted him victory, but instead he finds defeat through the trickery of a woman.

The song of Deborah is a declaration of the power of God and his support for his people, but it ends with the sad tale of Sisera's mother, reminding us of the very real loss that comes with war.

2 The call of Gideon

Judges 6:7–24

After the fine poetic hymn celebrating the victory of Deborah and Jael, this section of Judges focuses on the career of Gideon, the first of the judges to receive such an extended treatment. The cycle of success and failure for Israel continues. As a solution, God sends a prophet who reminds the people of the history of Israel in the exodus, proof of God's continued loyalty and a sign of Israel's need to follow him and no other god. It is a traditional statement on God's role and his requirements of Israel, but in a few verses Gideon will come and question that very role. We learn little about the prophet, in contrast to the importance placed on Deborah the prophetess in chapter 4.

It seems that the words of the prophet are not heeded and God must take direct action through the sending of a messenger or angel. The messenger comes to Gideon, who is threshing wheat secretly to prevent the Midianites from stealing it (v. 11). Given such circumstances, he naturally wonders where the fruits of all the promises from God are. His reaction is one that we may share: 'If God is with us, why do we have all these problems?' (v. 13). Gideon must test God, in a reversal of God's testing Israel. Gideon prepares an offering, which the messenger instructs him to place on a rock. The offering is consumed by fire and Gideon realizes that he has seen God face-to-face (v. 22). Moses too had seen God face-to-face, and Gideon is thus presented as a leader in the manner of Moses.

Gideon's response to this visit is to build an altar to the Lord (v. 24). This is significant since it is symbolic of his indecision. While he builds this altar, he is unwilling to tear down the altars to other gods, unaware that this is the root of Israel's problems. He must await God's instructions (v. 25) before he undertakes the destruction of the altars of Baal. Such indecision and failure to listen carefully to the words of God are at the heart of the problems for the people.

3 Gideon falters once more

Judges 6:33–40

Once more, Israel is in crisis, surrounded by its enemies. God emboldens Gideon through his Spirit (v. 34) and Gideon takes action by rallying the tribes of Israel. But he soon loses heart and must again test God, combining hesitancy with a degree of arrogance. While he does not have the confidence of faith to be sure that God will give him victory, he is bold enough to set a test himself for God, laying out the procedures. It is normally God who tests Israel, but Gideon again reverses the roles.

For the first test, Gideon places a fleece on the threshing floor, and in the morning there is dew on the fleece but not on the floor. Despite the success of the test, Gideon is not yet convinced and sets up another test—the opposite of the first. Next morning the floor is covered in dew but the fleece is dry. Gideon is aware that he is testing God too much, appealing to him not to be angry (v. 39). This second test could be seen as a parallel to God's test of Israel, leaving Israel unharmed by the nations round about, as the fleece remains untouched by dew.

The Bible includes many examples of people questioning or struggling with God, and Gideon's test, as well as reflecting the indecision within Israel, is a legitimate questioning of God. We are allowed to face up to God, to ask him why he is allowing things to happen, to challenge him. However, the questioning should always be part of our own submission to his will and a way for us to discover his intentions for us. This Gideon does, but he oversteps the mark. He has already tested God, and God has proven his loyalty. Yet Gideon needs to test him again—not just once but twice. He is aware that he has gone too far but he persists. He is a model of lack of faith, and this allows God to test him in return, by utilizing and mocking that lack of faith in the next chapter.

4 God's test

Judges 7:1–8

As Gideon and his troops prepare for battle, God decides that the army is too large. He devises a series of measures to reduce the numbers until there are only 300 soldiers left.

It is clear that God is showing his displeasure at Gideon's constant testing, and wishes to prove to Gideon once and for all that he can rely on him. The army is too large, which might cause Israel to think that victory was brought about by the success of the forces rather than the help of God. So God whittles down the army, and there could be no greater test for Gideon than to lead such a small army against the surrounding hostile forces. Gideon's tests, which were a matter of a wet or dry fleece, now seem trivial in the face of the reality of defeat at the hands of his enemies. God is proving that he can provide the ultimate test, one that he rather than Gideon chooses—and that he will pass it.

Why God chose those troops that lapped water like dogs (v. 5) is uncertain. It might be that those who stooped down to drink would have had to use their hands to scoop up the water, and would have been ill-prepared for fighting without their hands to the ready. It might also be that lapping like dogs is a humiliating position, and therefore that God chooses the lowliest and most unlikely people for his troops. It underlines the fact that Gideon is being given the smallest and meanest of armies imaginable. God has turned the tables on Gideon and is exploiting his weakness of lack of faith. This is the real trial for Gideon: can he really trust God even after so many of his own tests?

5 Gideon's victory

Judges 7:15–25

Following a dream-vision that promises victory, Gideon is emboldened and immediately commands his troops to rise up (v. 15), a decisive action from such a indecisive figure. The plan, as seen in his dream, is to capture the enemy's camp at its most vulnerable time. The Israelites are to strike when it is night, causing commotion precisely when the guards were changing duty—one lot being tired, the other still growing accustomed to the dark. The troops are commanded by Gideon to shout 'For God and Gideon!' (v. 17). This serves as a reminder that they are fighting for God, although it also contains a certain arrogance on Gideon's part that he is partially responsible for the victory.

The troops cause noise and confusion in the enemy camp, sounding horns and smashing jars. In case this was not enough, or in case we might think that this plan is too easy, God takes extra care. He ensures that, in the confusion, each man turns his sword against his fellows (v. 22), and the army flees. The confusion is so great that even loyal companions attack each other.

It is a great victory for Gideon and he conquers all the foreign tribes in the surrounding region, but it is a victory that contrasts with the earlier one of Deborah and Jael. Deborah, in her victory song, had ascribed all to God, and was unquestioning in what she needed to do. For Gideon, God had to orchestrate the whole situation while Gideon displayed uncertainty and lack of faith. Nevertheless, Gideon was still proud enough to have his troops call out 'For God and Gideon'. God had to prove that he was bringing about the victory through the reduction of the number of troops. Despite our own lack of faith and our hesitancy, God will provide and, no matter how many times we question or doubt God, as Gideon tested him, he will remain faithful to his word.

6 Death of Gideon

Judges 8:28–35

With the victory over Midian secured, the country again is peaceful, and this peace lasts some time (40 years) under Gideon. It is a fitting conclusion to the account of Gideon. The success of his leadership in military affairs is matched by his marital success. As well as having many wives (since polygamy was acceptable at the time), he was the father to 70 sons. Although 70 is a perfect number, and Gideon's prosperity is expressed in this fertility, the number 70 might also be symbolic for other reasons. It is the number of people who went down to Egypt with Joseph (Genesis 46:27), implying enough people to begin a nation. On a political level it is also the number of kings humiliated by Adoni-Bezek (Judges 1:7), indicating a complete league of tribes. Gideon is thus establishing the nation through his sons.

The reference to Gideon's concubine in verse 31 is obscure, since he might not have needed a concubine if he had many wives. The verse might be read as referring to one of his wives living in Shechem, but its importance lies in the mention of Shechem, where the next episode (ch. 9) is set.

Gideon's death is recounted in gentle terms—'in good old age'—and he is given the family honour of being buried in his father's tomb (v. 32), but this gentle description of the burial is interrupted by the immediate fall of Israel back into idolatry 'as soon as Gideon was dead'. Despite all the work of Gideon and the signs shown by God, the chapter ends with the same situation in which the book as a whole began. Israel no longer remembers God or even their recent judge, Gideon. The cycle continues: despite God's continued efforts, the people fail and God must seek a new way of bringing them back to him.

Guidelines

How do we decide what steps to take? This was a problem facing Gideon, and he chose a controversial method of testing God. At times we want to cry out to God, to complain to him or to question his very existence. It is often our way of expressing our own anger at failing to understand what purpose he has for us. Gideon is right to turn to God, but he takes it too far in trying a range of tests. God's response is to play on Gideon's weakness, forcing him to have the ultimate faith and lead to battle a handful of men. At times, trials confront us that take us to our limits, but we need to believe that we are doing the right thing. Crying out to God and wrestling with the problems, as Jacob wrestled with the angel in Genesis, can be not only a natural emotional response to difficulty but also a legitimate religious enterprise. Gideon found that it served him well and that, despite his indecision, God remained faithful and showed him the way forward.

The book of Judges is itself a test for us. It is an account of war and murder, in which God is ensuring success in battle for those who are loyal to him. Can God, then, countenance violence or war? There are no easy answers to this question, and discussions of whether a war can ever be just are prominent in the media today. A simple reading of the book that justifies war in the name of God is not helpful, but perhaps the book offers a different solution. Just as the characters are caught in a web of indecision, human failings and lack of faith, so we are naturally torn between different positions when faced with such questions. We need to struggle with God over these issues, testing and asking. Rather than providing a simple answer, the book of Judges presents the complexity of life and reveals the struggle behind every decision to be made. It is permitted to put God to the test, but only if we are willing to listen when the answer is offered.

FURTHER READING

Mieke Bal, *Death and Dissymmetry: The Politics of Coherence in the Book of Judges*, University of Chicago Press, 1988.

Athalya Brenner (ed.), *A Feminist Companion to Judges*, JSOT Press, 1993.

Lillian R. Klein, *The Triumph of Irony in the Book of Judges*, Almond, 1988.

Tammi J. Schneider, *Judges*, Liturgical Press, 2000.

CHRISTMAS: TIME FOR EVERYTHING

For some of us, this season signals chaotic busyness as we try to cram in all our card-writing, food-hoarding, party-going, gift-wrapping, before the shops close on Christmas Eve. For others, it is very much the opposite—a season that we will away, all too replete with unwanted space and difficult silence, invaded by the ghosts of Christmas past. In these last days of Advent and first days of Christmas, our daily readings are an invitation to listen deeply and to reflect on the way in which we live out this season. As we spend time with words of scripture and of familiar and not-so-familiar carols and poetry, we will seek to rediscover the reality that Christmas is in fact a time for everything. In the run-up to Christmas Day, we will take a look at some of the Old Testament passages that are traditionally understood to point to the coming of the Messiah. From Christmas Day onwards, we will focus on passages from the New Testament that draw us deeper into the significance of the nativity.

The miracle of Christmas allows us to live in the present, at peace with our limitations, recognizing that there is time enough for that which belongs and time to lay aside that which does not belong. The miracle of Christmas helps us to take a step towards acknowledging our memories, calling the treasures of the past into the present moment and recognizing in the present moment the beginning of future fulfilment. Augustine, in his *Confessions*, speaks of three times: 'The time of the past is memory, the time of the present is contemplation, and the time of the future is expectation. These three exist in the soul of the person—I see them nowhere else. In the innermost place of our humanity there exists no time—there it is pure present. There God allows us to discover our true selves.' May we find our way to the pure present this Christmas, as we celebrate the arrival of eternity in time.

Unless otherwise indicated, quotations are taken from the New Revised Standard Version.

1 Listen to the love song

Ecclesiastes 3:1–15

Yet with the woes of sin and strife
The world has suffered long:
Beneath the angels' strain have rolled
Two thousand years of wrong,
And man, at war with man, hears not
The love song which they bring:
O hush the noise, ye men of strife,
And hear the angels sing!
FROM 'IT CAME UPON A MIDNIGHT CLEAR', EDMUND H. SEARS (1810–76)

'It came upon a midnight clear' is a rather unusual Christmas carol. The grand descriptions speak of world, wars and angels, prophet-bards and an age of gold, while the name of Jesus goes unmentioned. But perhaps it is precisely this omission that gives the carol its powerful impact. All is tumult, conflict and activity as *the* decisive event in the history of the world takes place.

How can we ensure that we have not become deaf to the love song whose strains persist throughout world wars and ethnic conflicts, which plays on in spite of shopping mall musak and wall-to-wall sound? Today's passage gives us a clue: there is a time for everything and everything has its time. This assurance should help us to set aside the panic that says, 'Time is always insufficient—no matter what I am doing, I should always be somewhere else!' The set of seven plus seven pairs of activities (vv. 2–8) is an all-encompassing description of the process of living and dying. Ecclesiastes may be a difficult, at times cynical book, but here is a challenge to the compulsion to do everything now, and an invitation to trust the one in whose hand are all our times.

'And man at war with man hears not the love song which they bring.' These words were penned by a Unitarian minister who, rightly or wrongly, was accused of an inadequate Christology. The more important question for us today is whether we are overfamiliar with the name of Christ while oblivious to the love song of his arrival. What are you caught up in today? Ask God to give you his perspective on these preoccupations. Take some time now to be silent, and pray for a deepening of this silence during the days to come.

2 Blessed apple?

Genesis 3:1–15

Blessed be the time
That apple taken was;
Therefore we moun singen:
Deo gracias! Deo gracias! Deo gracias!
FROM 'ADAM LAY YBOUNDEN', ANONYMOUS

What is our perspective on the events of salvation history? The rubric over the reading from Genesis 3 in the traditional service of Nine Lessons and Carols betrays a retrospective interpretation of the significance of events in Eden: 'God declareth in the garden of Eden that the seed of woman shall bruise the serpent's head' (compare v. 15). This heading assumes the 'seed of woman' to refer to Christ himself. I wonder if the first Eve was able to see this far ahead?

The lines from 'Adam lay ybounden' also offer an intriguing perspective. They reflect the medieval doctrine of *felix culpa*, or blessed sin. The traditional Latin Mass and the *Exultet* of the Easter Vigil contain the words '*O felix culpa quae talem et tantum meruit habere redemptorem*' ('O happy fault that earned us so good and great a Redeemer'). If everything turns out all right in the end, can we be grateful even for sin? Without the fall of the first Adam, the birth of the last Adam would not have taken place. *Deo gracias!*

The strange logic of the caroler may make us chuckle, but it also invites us to reflect on the extent of the blessing that Christ's coming brings. As a result of the virgin birth at Bethlehem, the process is set in motion by which every single point in time will be redeemed. Even the darkest places of our history will be flooded with light (see Isaiah 9:2).

The tragedy of the first man and woman turning away from God in Eden was total. The decision to heed the serpent's suggestion was never and will never be a happy event. Yet, as a result of the work of Jesus, it may be seen quite differently, and this is what the caroler makes clear.

Genesis 3 also contains the beautiful description of the Lord God 'walking in the garden at the time of the evening breeze' (v. 8). The fall made such companionship a thing of the past. The incarnation has reinstated it as a possibility. Henri Nouwen has described Christmas as 'the renewed invitation not to be afraid and to let him—whose love is greater than our own hearts and minds can comprehend—be our companion'. Jesus is the promised 'Immanuel'—God with us, God walking alongside us. What are the things that you wish to share with God as you stroll with him today? What are the things that he wishes to share with you?

3 From ancient days

Micah 5:2–5

Of the Father's love begotten,
Ere the worlds began to be,
He is Alpha and Omega,
He the source, the ending He,
Of the things that are, that have been,
And that future years shall see,
evermore and evermore!
FROM 'OF THE FATHER'S LOVE BEGOTTEN', PRUDENTIUS AURELIUS (348–C.413),
TR. J.M. NEALE/H.W. BAKER

We might ask ourselves whether the wise men misquoted these words from Micah in their conversation with Herod in Matthew 2. While Micah's version speaks of Bethlehem diminutively, as 'one of the little clans of Judah' (v. 2), in Matthew she is 'by no means least among the rulers of Judah' (Matthew 2:6). It's an apparent discrepancy, but it reflects the dual reality that, though negligible in size, Bethlehem has a new and far-reaching significance as the birthplace of the Messiah.

We read backwards, from our 'post-nativity' perspective. How would Micah's original hearers have understood his message? One of the earliest of the minor prophets, Micah was active in the eighth century BC, during the reigns of Jotham, Ahaz and Hezekiah. He spoke out against social injustice and empty religion. Some have suggested that chapter 5 refers to the coming of the 'good king' Hezekiah, and indeed Hezekiah's reign was a golden age. He instituted far-reaching religious reform and we are told that 'there was no one like him among all the kings of Judah' (2 Kings 18:5). Yet when we look more closely at these verses, we find reference to one who is greater even than Hezekiah. This is a different category of Messiah altogether, 'whose origin is from of old, from ancient days' (v. 2). The Hebrew phrase here is employed of God in Psalm 90:2 and of God's wisdom in Proverbs 8:22–23.

A similar theme is picked up by Aurelius Prudentius, one of the last writers of the Roman empire, and one of the first Christian poets. His words offer us a powerful reflection on the one who is 'from everlasting to everlasting'. We may grow weary of the commercialism surrounding us at Christmas time. Apparently there is a conspiracy to put up the decorations earlier and remove them more promptly each year. In some quarters there is an attempt to remove Christ himself from Christmas and to reflect this in seasonal greetings and tinsel-decked snow scenes. Celebrating as we do a Messiah whose presence is for all people and for all time, our celebrations should be neither transient nor superficial. God's love for us in Christ is a love that encompasses all time. What implications does this have for the way in which we celebrate his coming today?

4 Treasure of nations

Haggai 2:1–9

Come, Thou long-expected Jesus,
Born to set Thy people free;
From our fears and sins release us;
Let us find our rest in Thee.
Israel's strength and consolation,
Hope of all the earth Thou art;

Dear desire of every nation,
Joy of every longing heart.
FROM 'COME, THOU LONG-EXPECTED JESUS', CHARLES WESLEY (1707–88)

Haggai 2 contains the Lord's encouragement to a people stuck in the past. In response to an earlier prophecy (1:1–11), they have commenced the work of rebuilding the temple. But already they are on the point of giving up: 'It'll never be anything like the old temple. Remember the fine craftsmanship, the gold and silver work. Why bother carrying on?' The Lord knows their thoughts, and names them (v. 3).

The reassurance they receive is very like the Immanuel promise that we will read tomorrow in Isaiah. 'Take courage... for I am with you' (v. 4). The role of God's people is not to dwell despondently on the past, but to continue obediently with the task they have been given to do, to the best of their ability and with the resources that are available. The Lord will do the rest. Although they may feel that their work is substandard and insignificant, he will use it to bring blessing to all nations. The new temple will have a splendour even greater than the former house, and in this place the Lord will 'give prosperity' (v. 9). The word translated 'prosperity' is *shalom*—peace, wholeness, perfection.

There was an immediate significance in these words for Zerubbabel, Joshua, Haggai and those who worked with them. They could take courage in the Lord's presence and persevere in the task they had been given to do. There was also a future significance, a pointer to the Messiah who was to come. 'And I will shake all nations, and the desire of all nations shall come: and I will fill this house with glory, saith the Lord of hosts' (v. 7, KJV). This rendering of Haggai 2:7 was the inspiration for Charles Wesley's lines quoted above. Wesley's carol serves as a prayer of invocation. Jesus has come, did come, two millennia ago. In praying this carol, we invite him to enter into the innermost places of our lives. He is all that we most need and long for. He is the fulfilment of our deepest desires. For the nations he is freedom, he is rest, he is strength and consolation. He is our hope, desire and joy.

5 Given, not lent

Given, not lent,
And not withdrawn—once sent,
This Infant of mankind, this One,
Is still the little welcome Son.
FROM 'UNTO US A SON IS GIVEN', ALICE MEYNELL (1847–1922)

Today we look at the first of four passages from Isaiah. The early verses of chapter 7 describe the discovery by Ahaz of Judah that the kings of Aram (Syria) and Israel have decided to join forces against him. We read that 'the heart of Ahaz and the heart of his people shook as the trees of the forest shake before the wind' (7:2). The Lord sends Isaiah to Ahaz to reassure him that neither the king of Syria nor the king of Israel will emerge victorious. Both kingdoms will be overcome by Assyria.

It seems that Ahaz is in need of further encouragement, for, in the passage we read today, the Lord also sends him the sign of a young woman who will bear a son and give him the name 'Immanuel'. As is so often the case, there is more than one 'layer' to this prophecy. It had an immediate significance for Ahaz in relation to his future and that of his people, but it is also taken up by Matthew centuries later as he reports the appearance of the angel of the Lord to Joseph, telling of the child who is to be born to Mary (Matthew 1:23).

Our reading from Isaiah begins with a question: 'Ask a sign of the Lord your God' (v. 11). With sophisticated 'I dare not' resolution, Ahaz refuses to put the Lord to the test (see Deuteronomy 6:16), but he has misunderstood the situation. This is not 'putting God to the test', but responding to the Lord's desire to give. Alice Meynell's poem is a beautiful reflection on the unconditional nature of the gift 'Immanuel'. It is also a reflection on childhood. A child is not afraid to ask, but how often adults are. 'Oh no, I couldn't—I couldn't possibly ask for anything!' But the Lord loves to bestow good gifts. In our early life he gives us innocence and security. He invites us to rejoice, delight and play. Our perspective and responsibilities change as we grow into adulthood, but the Christ-child with us is our reminder that the gifts and the invitation remain.

6 Wonderful child

Isaiah 9:2–7

Wondrous sight for men and angels!
Wonders, wonders without end!
He who made, preserves, sustains us,
He our Ruler and our Friend,
Here lies cradled in the manger,
Finds no resting-place on earth,
Yet the shining hosts of glory
Throng to worship at his birth.
FROM 'RHYFEDD, RHYFEDD GAN ANGYLION', ANN GRIFFITHS, TR. H.A. HODGES

We have turned on a couple of chapters in the book of Isaiah to a passage that describes the Lord's victory over Judah's oppressors. Specifically, we find mention of the newfound prosperity of the nation, the liberation from oppression and the end of conflict. As when Gideon led Israel to defeat the vast army of the Midianites (v. 4; see Judges 7:15–25), the people of Judah have been freed from Assyrian oppression. This has happened as a result of the birth of a child who has grown up to be a great king in the line of David. The events are related in the past tense, implying that this is not a prophecy about the future but a historical reality. Once again it would seem reasonable to infer a reference to good King Hezekiah. However, the names used in verse 6 present a tall order for any human king and, as we are reminded in 2 Chronicles 32:25, even Hezekiah failed to get it all right all of the time.

So, while in one sense this passage refers backwards to King Hezekiah as the agent of God's short-term rescue plan for the people of Judah, we also find ourselves looking forward to the one who can truly be described as 'Wonderful Counsellor, Mighty God, Everlasting Father and Prince of Peace'. It is a truth too vast to comprehend that the one who is worthy of this fourfold title can lie cradled in a manger, can be born as a vulnerable, helpless child.

The opening lines of 'Rhyfedd, rhyfedd gan angylion' are the exuberant expression of worship of one who was utterly overwhelmed by this truth.

Ann Griffiths was a tenant farmer's daughter from mid-Wales who died in relative obscurity in 1805, aged 29. These lines form the first verse of a plygain carol, laying out the whole sweep of salvation history in what has been described as one of the greatest religious poems in any language. In the words of Saunders Lewis, Ann is 'a poet of contemplation, a poet of the intellect, a poet who gazes outwards in wonder at the panorama of biblical truth'. Use her words to inspire you as you reflect on the splendour and perfection of God's plan for humankind.

Guidelines

Although the real Christmas story includes deprivation, forced migration and genocide, the way in which we mark the festival can cause us to airbrush out these details and to overlook similar circumstances where they exist in the world today. With some justification, we may opt for 'time out' from the bad news and switch channels when the crisis reports come on. The genius of G.K. Chesterton's 'Christmas carol' is that he manages to hold up the contentment, beauty and simplicity of the Christ-child alongside the conflicts and disillusionments of the world. Where the one encounters the other is the place of true *shalom*. Use Chesterton's poem as an inspiration in your prayers for the world today.

The Christ-child lay on Mary's lap,
His hair was like a light.
(O weary, weary were the world,
But here is all aright).

The Christ-child lay on Mary's breast,
His hair was like a star.
(O stern and cunning are the kings,
But here the true hearts are.)

The Christ-child lay on Mary's heart,
His hair was like a fire.
(O weary, weary is the world,
But here the world's desire.)

The Christ-child stood at Mary's knee,
His hair was like a crown.
And all the flowers looked up at him,
And all the stars looked down.
'A CHRISTMAS CAROL', G.K. CHESTERTON (1874–1936)

1 Shepherds' watch

Isaiah 11:1–10

Welcome, all wonders in one sight!
Eternity shut in a span!
Summer in winter! Day in night!
Heaven in earth! and God in man!
Great Little One, whose all-embracing birth
Lifts earth to heaven, stoops heaven to earth.
FROM 'AT BETHLEHEM', RICHARD CRASHAW (1613?–49)

These verses from Isaiah are cast in future time. They point us way beyond the reign of Hezekiah. We can recognize the stock, or stump, of Jesse as a reference to the house of David, and the shoot as the promised Messiah. From our perspective we can recall how the Spirit of the Lord alighted on Jesus at his baptism (Matthew 3:17), and we can think of all the demonstrations throughout Jesus' earthly ministry of his profound wisdom and understanding, counsel and might, knowledge and fear of the Lord.

The subsequent verses are more difficult. If verse 4 describes Jesus, then it is quite a different picture, more akin to the figure on the white horse in Revelation: 'From his mouth comes a sharp sword with which to strike down the nations, and he will rule them with a rod of iron' (Revelation 19:15). This is terrifying imagery, and yet we are not to fear, for his rule will be characterized by righteousness and equity. It will be a rule in which the whole of the natural order is turned on its head (vv. 6–10).

If Jesus has come, does this new order already exist? I have just been listening to a report about a group of bird watchers who were thrilled to sight, for the first time, a rare kind of swallow. Only seconds later, they watched in horror as a sparrowhawk swooped down and seized it. No, the wolf does not live with the lamb, and we cannot allow a toddler to play outside alone for even a few minutes, let alone near to a snake's hole. It would seem that we live in a time between the fulfilment of the first and second sections of the passage.

Are our times, then, 'between times'? In his poem 'At Bethlehem', an account of the shepherds' response to the nativity, Richard Crashaw conveys a sense of how the coming of Christ collapses our concept of time and turns our ideas and expectations upside down. Perhaps, as years go by, you find yourself fearing the passing of time. Ask God to give you a new perspective as you reflect on Isaiah's vision today.

2 Come tomorrow

Isaiah 22:20–25

O come, thou Key of David, come
And open wide our heavenly home;
Make safe the way that leads on high,
And close the path to misery.
FROM 'O COME, O COME, EMMANUEL', ANONYMOUS, TR. J.M. NEALE (1818–66)

Of all the Old Testament texts that have been regarded as messianic prophecies, this passage from Isaiah is surely the strangest. It focuses solely on the Lord's servant Eliakim, son of Hilkiah. Eliakim is a court official under King Hezekiah. He is to be called to replace Shebnah, who has proved a disgrace to his master's house (22:18). The Key of David in these verses is undeniably Eliakim. We could not justifiably make the connection with Jesus had Jesus not assumed the title for himself. The following is Jesus' own introduction to his words through John on Patmos to the church at Philadelphia: 'These are the words of the holy one, the true one, who has the key of David, who opens and no one will shut, who shuts and no one opens' (Revelation 3:7).

'O come, thou Key of David' is one of an ancient series of antiphons that were used in the medieval church liturgy in the week leading up to Christmas. Each antiphon contains one of the messianic titles ascribed to Jesus: *Sapientia* (Wisdom: Isaiah 11:2), *Adonai* (Lord of Might: Exodus 19:16), *Radix Jesse* (Root of Jesse: Isaiah 11:10), *Clavis David* (Key of David: Isaiah 22:22), *Oriens* (Dayspring/Morning Star: Numbers 24:17), *Rex gentium* (King/Desire of Nations: Haggai 2:7), *Emmanuel* (Emmanuel: Isaiah 7:14). You might like to spend some time looking up the Old Testament reference for each antiphon and praying through any that are especially pertinent to your current situation. Note that the initial letters of the Latin antiphons taken in reverse order spell *ero cras*, or 'I will be [with you] tomorrow'—a marvellous promise for Christmas Eve.

Jesus tells the Christians at Philadelphia, 'I have set before you an open door, which no one is able to shut' (Revelation 3:8). The Key of David antiphon is a powerful assurance for those who are facing persecution for their faith, who are beset by doubts, or for whom this Christmas feels like the dark valley rather than the hilltop experience that others suggest it should be. No matter what we may be going through, the Key of David is our guarantee that even this path will lead to an infinitely better place.

3 Security and danger

Luke 2:1–7

I saw a stable, low and very bare,
A little child in a manger.
The oxen knew him, had him in their care,
To men he was a stranger.
The safety of the world was lying there,
And the world's danger.
'SALUS MUNDI', MARY COLERIDGE (1861–1907)

Christmas Day has arrived and these familiar verses from Luke sound different today. The baby has been born and we can celebrate. There are a number of Christmas carols that seek to paint the nativity scene through the eyes of the shepherds. In her short poem, Mary Coleridge does not make it clear whose perspective she has taken. Is she so caught up in the events of Christmas that she can imagine herself there, describing the scene before her? What is it that she perceives?

The first few lines do not present us with anything very new or striking. She mentions stable *and* manger, which is quite in keeping with famous paintings and Christmas cribs. In fact, the Gospels contain only the one word *phatne*, meaning the place where animals feed, so we could equally well imagine a trough in the middle of a field under the stars or a cave where there is fodder and shelter. The second option would be in keeping with an ancient tradition going back to the apologist Justin (c. AD150).

It must have taken a great deal of planning on God's part to ensure that the Messiah was indeed born in the City of David. Why did Joseph deem it necessary to take Mary on an 80-mile journey nine months into her pregnancy? Presumably to protect her from gossiping tongues: 'She had an encounter with an angel? Yeah, and my name's Augustus Caesar...' Talking of Caesar, his calling of the census must have been part of God's plan too. Historians have done all manner of mental gymnastics to tally the dating of the known years of census with Mary and Joseph's journey, and with the years when Quirinius was governing Syria. Even if Luke made some mistakes in his dating, God did not, for these unlikely events coincided, with the result that the birth took place in Bethlehem *a là* Micah 5:2.

The last two lines of Mary Coleridge's poem are the most striking. This child spells safety *and* danger. Remember the righteous judge of Isaiah 11? Remember the words of the prophet Simeon to Mary (Luke 2:34)? To what extent have we 'sanitized' our understanding and expectations of Jesus? As Mr Beaver said of Aslan in the Narnia stories, 'He's not a tame lion.'

4 Child for us

Galatians 4:4–6

Child in the manger,
infant of Mary;
outcast and stranger,
Lord of all:

child who inherits
all our transgressions,
all our demerits
on him fall.

FROM 'LEANABH AN AIGH', MARY MACDONALD (1789–1872),
TR. LACHLAN MACBEAN (1853–1931)

We have travelled the Advent journey. The long-awaited has arrived. The gift has been given and the gift wrappings lie strewn on the floor all around us. But as we look forward, how can we ensure that we do not just 'box up' this celebration and save it for another year?

Paul gives some guidance in Galatians 4. In a few carefully chosen words, he reminds us what God has done and why he has done it. His opening sounds credal, something that we can affirm and believe in (v. 4). Yet there is much more. Here are some comments from a sermon preached by Martin Luther on Christmas Day 1531, which help us connect the what with the why.

In order to understand this article of faith: Conceived by the Holy Spirit and born of the Virgin Mary, we are always to add 'For us'. For whom was he conceived and born? For whom did he suffer and die? For us, for us, for us! Always add us! … Christ didn't need these works. He would have remained a lord quite well without them. Rather, his conception and birth, his suffering and death, his ascension and sitting at the right hand are all for our benefit. They belong to us. Note that well!

God has sent his Son for us. He has sent a child so that we might become his children. Many centuries after the birth in Bethlehem, another Mary composed a carol about the first Mary's child. A young Gaelic-speaking countrywoman, living near Bunessan on the Isle of Mull, wrote of an infant who from the very outset was 'outcast and stranger'. His rejection was the necessary route to our salvation—a strange and scandalous truth, but our reality.

God has sent a child so that we might become his children, that we might receive the Spirit of his Son who enables us to cry out 'Abba! Father!' We have two choices: we can either observe the Christmas story from without, perceiving it to be a beautiful and moving narrative, or we can enter fully into it, because we recognize that it is *our* story, that this extraordinary story is entirely for us.

5 In a nutshell

1 Timothy 3:16

A little child,
A shining star,
A stable rude,
The door ajar,
Yet in this place,
So crude, forlorn,
The Hope of all
The world was born.
ANONYMOUS

T.S. Eliot describes the incarnation as 'the intersection of the timeless with time'. We have already seen that the coming of Jesus has a strange effect on time. What is the temporal perspective from which Paul writes his pithy saying in 1 Timothy 3:16? Is he referring to past events or to future fulfilment? Has he got the order of events muddled up? Is Jesus 'believed in throughout the world' or is this reality still to come?

A detailed phrase-by-phrase exegesis of this particular verse is unlikely to help very much. We need to lay chronologies aside and regard what we have read as a kind of poem, intended to be memorized and repeated, enjoyed and marvelled over. Just as the anonymous poem above gives the nativity story in a nutshell, this verse gives us the whole of the Christian gospel in a nutshell. At the most basic level, the first two lines remind us that Jesus lived a human life, and that he died for us and rose again. The second pair of lines reminds us that he sits in heaven in the presence of the angels, yet is made known to people on earth. The final pair of lines gives an indication of present reality: as Jesus now rules in heaven, those on earth are placing their lives in his hands. Yet there is much more, so much more, and we will only begin to appreciate how much if we allow these words to take root in our hearts. This poem is one for holding up to the situations we encounter in our daily lives. It gives us a story by which to shape our own. Spend a couple of minutes learning these words for yourself now, and resolve to repeat and reflect further on them during the days to come.

6 Back to the present

1 John 4:7–21

Love shall be our token,
Love be yours and love be mine,
Love to God and all men,
Love for plea and gift and sign.
FROM 'LOVE CAME DOWN AT CHRISTMAS', CHRISTINA ROSSETTI (1830–94)

Christina Rossetti's profound carol echoes what John is teaching here. Love is never exclusive. There is not one love for God and another for our brothers and sisters. If we are without love for our siblings, we are without love for God. This is a difficult teaching, particularly at those times when we feel frustration, annoyance or anger towards those around us. At such times we need to choose the way of love. We need to take hold of that which originates not in our own half-hearted efforts, but in God's revelation to us in Christ, for Jesus is God's love made visible.

In this series of readings, we have thought about time and the nature of time. We have considered Augustine's definition of the pure present and reflected on our means of entry into it. The invitation into the pure present is also an invitation to lay down the burdens of fear about the future and regrets concerning the past. Letting go of the past can be a long and painful process. The Lord says, 'Abide in my love' (John 15:9). John gives us a powerful demonstration of why we need have no fear of what is to come (1 John 4:17). He also reminds us of the purifying potential of God's perfect love (v. 18).

What thoughts are contained in the last line of Rossetti's carol? Love is our plea. A plea is offered by a defendant in a court of law. We have a perfect plea and need not fear judgment. Love is our gift—a gift that we have received, but also one that we have the opportunity to give to others. How many hours did you spend battling the crowds in the pre-Christmas rush, agonizing over what to buy for a loved one? Here is the perfect gift: let us pray that God will show us how to do the giving. Love is our sign. A sign can be something quite simple, humble, accessible. We may feel that this sign—the love that we are able to show—is very small, yet it points to a reality infinitely greater than our ability to comprehend.

Guidelines

Spend some time exploring these lines from another of G.K. Chesterton's poems. What are your reflections at the end of this series of readings? What have you learned, experienced or gained this Christmas? What will you take with you as you journey on into the present? Will you journey as a wise man or as a little child?

Go humbly, humble are the skies,
And low and large and fierce the Star;
So very near the Manger lies
That we may travel far.

Hark! Laughter like a lion wakes
To roar to the resounding plain.
And the whole heaven shouts and shakes,
For God Himself is born again,
And we are little children walking
Through the snow and rain.

From 'The wise men', G.K. Chesterton (1874–1936)

NEW YEAR AND THE PSALMS

What do you think about at New Year? The year that has just passed? The year that is about to start? Your New Year resolutions? One of the interesting features of the Christian tradition is that Christianity does not have any particular theological themes associated with New Year. In this, as in many other ways, we can learn something from Jewish tradition and from the Old Testament. At *Rosh HaShana*, the Jewish festival of New Year that takes place in the autumn, the major theme of the prayers and worship is God's kingship and rule over the world. Many Old Testament scholars trace this emphasis on God's kingship and action in creation back to the worship of ancient Israel in the temple. In ancient Israel, one of the major festivals was the feast of Tabernacles, which celebrated the gathering in of the final harvest of the year. Various scholars believe that the feast of Tabernacles also marked the New Year festival and at this festival the kingship of God and his rule over creation were celebrated. The Psalms that we will be looking at this week have all been associated with this possible ancient New Year festival.

How better to bring in the New Year than by being firmly focused on God's wonderful, awesome reign in creation, which we can trace day by day in the world around us? This theme offers us an enriched sense of God's presence in our life as we start out on a new year with God.

1 How great thou art!

Psalm 29

Do you have a favourite hymn? Many people love the hymn 'How great thou art' and, as a result, it appears at the top of a number of charts for our top ten favourite hymns. It sums up the feeling of overwhelming awe that we can experience when we encounter the wonders of creation and think about God's role as Creator. Psalms like Psalm 29 are the Old Testament equivalent of this hymn. In it our attention is focused on God's greatness and power over creation. In the Septuagint (the Greek translation of the Old Testament), the title at the start of the psalm associates it with the feast of Tabernacles, and so possibly also with the New Year. It is also thought to be one of the oldest psalms in the Psalter. This illustrates that our ancient ancestors in the faith had similar feelings of awe at God's majesty.

Somewhat surprisingly, however, the ones called to celebrate God's greatness are not human beings. Those summoned in verse 1 are literally 'sons of gods', translated variously in English as 'ye mighty' (KJV), 'Sons of the mighty' (NAS), 'O mighty ones' (NIV), 'Sons of God' (NJB) and 'heavenly beings' (RSV). This is because translators are not quite sure what to do with the phrase. Most scholars think that angels are being addressed here, and this may well be because, in the rest of the psalm, God's greatness is seen to be so important that only angels can adequately begin to express it.

Another feature of this psalm is the phrase 'the voice of God', which occurs seven times. This has caused one commentator to call Psalm 29 the 'Psalm of Seven Thunders', because of the fact that God's voice was associated with thunder in the Old Testament. What we see, then, is a picture of God who is both in charge of the world in which we live and responsible for what happens within it. Notice that this is both reassuring and frightening: God's voice breaks trees, shakes the desert and wipes out forests as well as being 'over the flood'. This powerful, awesome God causes all those in heaven to cry out 'Glory!' On earth we echo this cry in our own way, and that is why 'How great thou art' remains such a popular hymn.

2 A very present help

Psalm 46

Psalm 29 reminded us of the awesomeness of the Creator God who can rip out trees and shake the desert. In this psalm, we are reminded of how reassuring the greatness of God can be. Fear and comfort go hand in hand in the Psalms: the God who is powerful enough to have absolute control over the whole of creation is also the God who is powerful enough to protect us when we need it. Psalm 46 speaks strongly of this God who shelters the people from harm and gives them strength. God is also, in the

NRSV translation, 'a very present help in trouble' (v. 1). This is a poetic rendition but it misses some of the depth of meaning. In Hebrew, the verse means literally 'a helper in trouble he has been found very much'. The NRSV misses the sense that God's action as a shelter and source of strength is assured because, over and over again in the past, God has been there when help is needed. This is the very basis of our faith and certainty in God: both in our own lives and in the pages of the Bible we see God's presence in times of trouble and know that God will be present again.

The psalm goes on to talk of the way in which Jerusalem, God's holy city, is established firmly and protected by God. In the midst of the chaos of daily life—the raging of the sea and earthquakes (vv. 2–3), coups and wars (v. 6)—God is there, the still centre in a world of chaos and destruction. Our task as God's people, then, is to find that still centre and, in the words of verse 10, 'be still, and know that I am God'. Twice in the psalm (vv. 7, 11), the refrain 'the Lord of hosts is with us; the God of Jacob is our refuge' is used, reminding and reassuring us that God is by our side as in the past and sheltering us from harm.

If you have not quite completed your list of New Year resolutions, perhaps you could add verse 10 to them. Make it a daily resolution to remind yourself of these words: 'be still and know that I am God'. A year shot through with stillness and the knowledge of God's presence must surely be a good one!

3 God has gone up with a shout

Psalm 47

Psalm 47 brings us back once again to the glorious kingship of God. The psalm falls into two sections with two introductory verses (vv. 1, 6), which are then expanded in what comes after them (vv. 2–5, 7–10). The two introductory verses instruct the people of God in how they should respond to the news of God's kingship: they should clap their hands, shout to God (v. 1) and sing praises (v. 6). The amazing news of God's kingship over the earth seems to require the production of as much noise as possible: the clapping, shouting and singing are joined in verse 5 by the sound of trumpets. One of the challenges for us in reading this psalm is to ask what kind of response we give to the news of God's kingship in the world. While some people feel entirely comfortable stamping, clapping and singing of God's kingship, others do not. What is important, however, is that you celebrate God's kingship, not how you do it.

Some scholars have tried to understand a little of what might have gone on at the New Year festival from psalms such as this one. One particularly important reference is in verse 5, where the psalmist says that God has gone up with a shout and with the sound of a trumpet. Some understand this to refer to a procession taking the ark of the covenant, which symbolized God's presence on earth, into the temple; others tie it more with the person of the king, who might have represented God on occasions such as these; still others think that it refers to God himself ascending into heaven. Whatever practices it referred to in ancient Israel, this psalm reminds us of the importance of gathering together, of giving thanks for God's kingship over the whole earth and of praising God. God's kingship demands that we respond with praise: how we do it is up to us.

4 The Lord is king

Psalm 93

In Psalm 47 we gained a glimpse of how the ancient Israelites might have worshipped God at a New Year festival. Psalm 93 has been used by scholars to give us another glimpse of what the New Year festival might have looked like. In this psalm, alongside the reference to God being king are references to the robe of God (v. 1) and the throne of God (v. 2). For many years, scholars have debated whether or not this refers to a ritual that could have taken place in the New Year festival, in which the king was enthroned as a symbol of God's enthronement over the entire world. If the proponents of this theory are correct, it means that God was symbolically being enthroned each year at the festival, in order to remind people not only of the significance of his kingship and but also of the fact that the human king was ruling for him.

Another part of this and other similar psalms, often cited to support this theory, are the first few words: 'The Lord reigns'. They can also be translated as 'YHWH is king' or 'YHWH has become king', and this last version is the one favoured by those who see an enthronement festival lying behind such psalms.

The practices of ancient Israel no longer take place, and we will never know what actions accompanied these psalms, but their sentiment remains ringing clearly across the centuries. The world as we know it has been established and maintained by God the king. Indeed, the very foundations of the world as we know it today were shaped by God's separation of the waters of the flood in Genesis 1. These floods, the psalmist maintains, were majestic and powerful (v. 3); how much more majestic, then, must be the one who separated them in the first place for creation to take place. God is indeed more majestic than anything else we can imagine on earth, and yet cares so deeply about the world he created that he stays intimately involved with everything that happens in it.

5 A new song

Psalm 96

Like the other psalms that we have been studying this week, Psalm 96 celebrates God's kingship and calls upon the whole of creation to do the same. The psalm falls into four sections. The first three verses call upon the whole of creation to sing to God in praise for everything that he has done for us. We, as well as the mountains, sea and trees, should sing songs about God's salvation and the marvellous things he has done on the earth. Such a command offers an important structure for our spiritual devotions. It is very easy to get caught up in the day-to-day concerns and anxieties of our lives. Even when those concerns are huge and crucially important, this psalm reminds us to look more widely than just at our own circumstances, and to remember what God has done in creation, in history for the people of God and in each one of our lives. Not only are we to remember and sing about it but to proclaim it 'among the nations': when we call to mind the many things God has done, we should not be able to keep our gratitude to ourselves!

The rest of the psalm expands on the initial section. The second section (vv. 4–6) answers the question, 'Why should we do this?' We should do it because God is God and no one else is; the other 'gods' are simply blocks of wood but this God, our God, created the world. The third section expands again (vv. 7–9): not only should we sing to God and proclaim him to the world, but we should also ascribe to God those qualities that he deserves to have—glory and strength. In other words, we need to recognize what God has by right.

Notice the way in which the poetry works: in verses 1–3 and 7–9 there are three lines to each section, two of which begin with the same word and the third of which is different. So in verses 1–3 we have 'Sing', 'Sing' and 'Declare'; in verses 7–9 there is 'Ascribe', 'Ascribe' and 'Worship'. The third word moves us on from the first two and shows us their purpose.

The final section of the psalm records the response of the earth to our proclamation of God: the physical world will respond with joy to our proclamation. The question that remains unanswered at the end of this psalm, packed with joyfulness, is 'How will humanity react?'

6 Holy and forgiving

Psalm 99

Our last psalm this week is also the last enthronement psalm in the Psalter. Like all the others, it focuses on our praise of God who is king over the whole world. Alongside these now familiar themes, however, we find a new theme emphasized in this psalm: the holiness of God. In many of the other psalms we have studied, God's holiness has been understood but not stated explicitly. Here we find the word repeated three times: 'Holy is he' (vv. 3, 5) and 'God is holy' (v. 9).

As the surrounding verses make clear, the holiness of God is wonderful but also terrifying: it causes us to extol God but also to quake. The Hebrew word for 'holy' has the meaning of separation, of something that is set apart. The Hebrew tradition stresses the fact that God is too holy for normal earthly events, so the place (the temple) and people (the priests) nearest to God must remain set apart themselves and hence worthy of God's presence. The sacrificial system was put in place to wipe out the impurities that offended God's holiness and kept him away from the people.

This emphasis is brought out in the second half of Psalm 99, where it talks of some of the eminent people of the past who were close to God: Moses, Aaron and Samuel (v. 6). The implication of what is written here is that God is too holy to have anything to do with us mortal creatures but, because God is willing to forgive us, he will still listen to us as he did to them. Within the New Testament, this theme becomes even more

135

important because of the incarnation of Jesus, who, despite his own holiness, was prepared to walk in the midst of the people and, even more than that, to seek out the impure outcasts of society. God is a holy God but he does not use this holiness to hide away from us.

Guidelines

This week we have had a feast of praise. Over and over again, the awesome wonder, the immense holiness, the glorious majesty and the marvellous acts of God have been laid out and celebrated in these psalms that many people associate with the ancient Israelite New Year festival. They are the biblical equivalent of fireworks, and you can almost hear the 'ooohs and aaahs' of delight that accompany the best firework displays as God's immense, powerful presence is celebrated in our midst.

Of course, the problem with fireworks is that they distract us from the harsh realities of life. I don't know how you felt as we read through these psalms but, in the back of my mind, I couldn't help but ask questions. Yes, God is a wonderful creator, and God shelters us in our time of need, but what about those who are not sheltered? What about those who experience more of the terror of God than of God's loving kindness? What about those who are drowned in the flood or crushed by the falling trees? These psalms deliberately focus on the wonder of God's action in the world but there is another side—the side that trembles before a raging God, the side that shouts at the God who appears to take no notice. You don't have to read around the psalms very far before you encounter this other side represented as clearly as the side we have been looking at this week.

The wonderful thing about the Psalms is that we have the glorious celebrations of God's majesty alongside the angry, bitter psalms of lament. We have been focusing on one aspect of a broad spectrum that runs through the whole of the book of Psalms. The fireworks do not deny the harsh reality of life; they take their place alongside them. We need both to grow and thrive as God's people in this wonderful world that he created.

The BRF

Magazine

Richard Fisher writes...

Open the Bible at random in a few places and you'll soon notice how many different types of writing it contains: poetry, prose, lists of names and numbers, dialogue and letters can all be found there. Some parts of it will draw you in immediately, while others may be frankly off-putting, at least at first sight.

At BRF, we've identified one of our core ministries as helping people to explore the Bible with confidence. All explorers going into unknown territory feel happier about the task if they have the right equipment—clothing and tools—to tackle every kind of environment they might encounter. BRF's books aim to do that for intrepid Bible readers—to make them equipped for all terrain.

This issue of the *BRF Magazine* kicks off with Henry Wansbrough's whistlestop tour of the whole Bible, spotlighting different parts in quick succession and providing insights into their origin and purpose. Later, Naomi Starkey suggests four ways of plotting a course through the various biblical books with the aid of the *People's Bible Commentary*. Whatever kind of journey you want to take, the PBC can provide you with a good map.

Not all explorers cover vast tracts of land, however, and exploring the Bible needn't mean trying to read the whole library that it contains. Naomi also recommends two books that focus more closely —one on the glory of Jesus in the Gospel of John and the other on what today's emerging church can learn from the first-century church at Antioch, home base for Paul's expeditions in the book of Acts.

We also have an extract from BRF's Advent book for 2007, discovering the 'beginnings and endings' encompassed by the Christian story, and a taster of Adrian Plass's revised and expanded edition of his bestselling collection of daily readings, *When You Walk*.

Finally, Lucy Moore gives us her insights into the excitement of opening up the special character of the Bible with primary school children, and explains how you can help with this huge task.

I hope you'll find something here to encourage you to set off on a new exploration of the Bible, confident that you're well equipped for whatever you discover on the journey.

Richard Fisher, Chief Executive

Bible salad

Henry Wansbrough OSB

I'm quite a serious sort of person, and when I read a book I like to learn something from it, something that helps me to understand a bit more about myself, my character and motivation, or about other people and their difficulties and achievements, or about the world and life in general. So I read a novel about an autistic child or about the difficulties that gradually poison a marriage. A biography will also do, to see how a general honed his skills or a bishop mastered his temper or a poet came to love the richness of life.

The Jews and early Christians collected many different sorts of writings that spoke to them about the ways of God. The Jews put them together and called them the Bible. The early Christians added more writings, which showed them what they considered to be the crowning end of the story. In one way it had already happened and in another it was still eagerly expected. All these writings added to their knowledge of God and of God's dealings with the world.

Even the writings of the New Testament show a great deal of variety. Don't open the New Testament without preparing for a bumpy ride! The writing starts, of course, with the letters that Paul wrote to various communities, all of which except the community at Rome, that awesome capital of empire, he had founded. To the Romans he shows great respect, as a provincial writing to the mighty city, hardly daring to offer them advice. To his much-loved community at Philippi (the only community from which he would accept gifts of money) he is affectionate and intimate. To his friend Philemon, the owner of his slave-helper Onesimus, he is playful and light-hearted, punning on Onesimus' name, which means 'Useful'. All of these were written long before the Gospels came into their present shape. After them come those two great letters, Colossians and Ephesians, which were perhaps not penned by Paul, but may be first fruits of his teaching and training, developing aspects of his own letters and applying his message to the situation of Christians a few years later.

At a certain stage, some community must have asked an unknown catechist named Mark to gather up and put together the oral traditions that had long been circulating in the communities. Why Mark? Because he was a brilliant storyteller, writing admittedly in primitive Greek, but with a sophisticated plan that brings out the charismatic personality of Jesus and the ever-increasing amazement of the people who could not help but see God at work in him. Soon afterward, two communities were not wholly satisfied with this portrait, wanting more of Jesus' teaching to be recorded. One, a community of Christians of Jewish origin, asked Matthew to give a fuller account against the background of Jesus' Jewish roots.

Another community, notably more affluent and settled in the milieu of the Greco-Roman empire, asked Luke to show them how Jesus and his message should be seen from their point of view. Luke had a genius for expressing a theological message through storytelling. Just look at the scene of the annunciation to Mary or the parable of the good Samaritan! He also wrote a second volume about the early years of the Christian community and about Paul's missionary journeys. This 'Acts of the Apostles' tells the story brilliantly, making the most of those favourite features of novels and histories of the time—riot scenes, escapes from prison, court appearances, shipwreck—not to mention the carefully worked speeches put into the mouths of the leading characters.

In a class by itself is the Gospel of John, seemingly almost entirely independent of the other Gospels, more developed theologically (but not necessarily therefore later). The 'beloved disciple' who stands behind this tradition dwells lovingly on the affection and human responsiveness of Jesus. The stories are fewer but are told with tranquillity and humour. Chiefly John struggles to show what it can mean to say that Jesus is fully divine. He has in every way the powers and dynamic of God. He is the Word of God made flesh.

In a class by itself is the Gospel of John

A wholly different sort of writing is strangely related to this author: the Revelation of John. It issues from the world of fierce persecution of Christians who would not join in the cult of the Roman emperors, assuring them—in the lurid symbolism of blood and cosmic collapse—that they would eventually triumph before the still higher throne of God and the Lamb.

If the types of writing in the New Testament are varied, those of the Old Testament are kaleidoscopic. Let us run backwards chronologically for a moment! The later writings range from the intense and agonized drama of Job's stalwart but trusting complaints at his undeserved suffering to the humorous novelette of the book of Tobit (in the Apocrypha), which at once honours and makes fun of the fussy exactitude of the old man's legal observance. The Wisdom literature ranges from the sage counsel and neat certainties of that learned scribe Ben Sira (again, Apocryphal) to the puzzled paradoxes of Qoheleth (Ecclesiastes), who poses as King Solomon himself. Even the prophets alone range from Isaiah's sublime and awe-inspired celebration of the Holy One of Israel to the self-critical humour of Jonah, the disobedient Jew who grumbles at God's acceptance of the obedience of the Gentiles. And in the Psalms all our own moods of prayer can be found, from dire complaint at unjustified (or, indeed, justified) persecution to tranquil or jubilantly noisy praise of the glory of God.

The backbone of the earlier part of the Old Testament is the history of God's gradual formation of his people of Israel, as he pats them into shape through thick and thin—and there is plenty of both. This account makes use of all kinds of material, from the oral folk-history of the patriarchs, half-lost in the mists of time, the shifting sands of the exodus, which celebrate in imagery of thunder and earthquake the first awesome experience of God claiming Israel for his own. Then, some unknown author in exile in Babylon drew together the memories and records (some being stories to account for an age-old ruin, others being exact court records) of the centuries in Canaan. He shaped them to show that Israel's constant unfaithfulness won her the loving chastisement of God, until God could tolerate it no longer and had to suffer the shame of abandoning his people to the savagery of other peoples, serving other gods. And behind it all, right at the beginning, stand those crucial first chapters of Genesis, which almost predict what is going to happen. They analyse in story form the relationship of the world to its Creator, the grandeur and the weakness of the human creature, the ineradicable human tendency to failure when left unaided.

All these different kinds of writing were needed to express God's word, assailing first one ear, then another, in the different circumstances of each. In any case, the Bible is never dull… well, hardly ever. You may even find the prescriptions in Leviticus for the treatment of leprosy fascinating, but —unless you operate with a large-scale map of the Near East—the genealogies of Chronicles will surely provoke a yawn!

Henry Wansbrough OSB leads a course for MA in Theology at Ample-forth Abbey in Yorkshire. He is a Series Editor for The People's Bible Commentary *and the author of* Luke *in that series.*

The Editor recommends

Naomi Starkey

As Christians we believe that the Bible presents the story of God's dealings with his creation and with us, his creatures. Beginning with—literally—the very beginning, scripture takes us from the first act of rebellion in Eden and on through the unfolding of God's great rescue plan, culminating in the coming of Jesus, Messiah, Saviour of the world (and, as we know, it does not end there). We return to it again and again, studying, pondering, seeking prayerfully to discover fresh insights from its pages.

Jesus' life, death and resurrection are, of course, the supreme focus of the four Gospels, and it is there that we can turn to seek answers to the question, 'Just what exactly is so special about Jesus and what he accomplished during his life and ministry?' Even if we have not asked ourselves this question with any urgency, we will encounter it as we share our faith with others.

Focusing on just one of the Gospels is a good way of 'soaking' ourselves in who Jesus is and the significance of what he has done. *Meeting the Saviour* takes as its focus the Gospel of John, and demonstrates how its particular emphasis is on exploring the glory of Jesus, as revealed in his life, his teaching, his death and his impact on human history.

Author Derek Tidball shows how 'glory' is one of the themes of this Gospel, alongside 'light', 'life' and

'truth'. In a series of straightforward and accessible Bible-based reflections, he takes key stories and teaching in the Gospel account, showing how they portray Jesus' time on earth as, in effect, one long transfiguration. This revealed, to those able and willing to see it, the glory that is the signature of God in creation.

The book works chapter by chapter through the many different episodes and impressions of Jesus that appear in John's Gospel, considering how the apostle shaped the narrative to elucidate this theme of glory. We see Jesus as sacrificial lamb, wise teacher, eternal word, sabbath breaker, good shepherd, true vine, dying king and hope restorer, among a host of other examples. As we ponder these passages, we too can meet the Saviour, allowing ourselves to be transformed by his touch.

Derek Tidball is Principal of the

London School of Theology and was previously Head of the Mission Department at the Baptist Union of Great Britain. He has written and contributed to many books, including most recently *The Message of Leviticus* (IVP, 2005), *Wisdom from Heaven* (Christian Focus, 2003), and *The Message of the Cross* (IVP, 2001).

The transformation we experience when we encounter the risen Jesus needs to flow out into our worship and witness. As the Church, particularly in the West, struggles against decades of decline, the call has gone out to develop 'emerging churches' and 'mission-shaped' initiatives. Instead of simply attending the same old services in the same old way, Christians must work to ensure that their witness remains both prophetic and challenging—but also relevant to a rapidly changing culture. Somehow we must find ways of relating to today's world without watering down the gospel message.

Ray S. Anderson is senior professor of theology and ministry at Fuller Theological Seminary, California, known worldwide for cutting edge theological and mission thinking. In *An Emergent Theology for Emerging Churches*, he explores the parallels between the situation facing the church today and the first-century Antioch church, where the apostle Paul shaped what could be described as 'emergent theology', developing from the 'parent' Jerusalem church.

It is inspiring reading for church leaders involved in any kind of 'mission-shaped' initiative—and all those concerned about how we bear witness to the gospel today. Yes, we need to shape what we say so that our intended audience can hear our message. At the same time, though, we can heed the author's assurance that this is not about a new theology but about re-envisioning 'a vintage theology—the same, yesterday, today and forever. It is about a theology that sings as well as stings, igniting the mind and stirring the heart'.

His argument centres on the fact that what is important is building Christ-centred communities, which bear witness by what they do as much as what they say, and where the focus is on the Holy Spirit rather than just 'spirituality'. At the same time, the emphasis needs to be on mission as well as ministry, and about looking to what lies ahead and not simply pondering on what has passed into history.

A book that provides much food for thought as well as stimulus for action, *An Emergent Theology for Emerging Churches* has been warmly endorsed by a number of leading figures including Eddie Gibbs, Professor of Church Growth at Fuller Theological Seminary, Brian McLaren, and Todd Hunter, National Director of Alpha USA.

To order a copy of Meeting the Saviour *or* An Emergent Theology for Emerging Churches*, please turn to the order form on page 159.*

An extract from
Beginnings and Endings

Advent is all about beginnings—the beginning of the Church year, of creation, of Christianity, and of the new heavens and the new earth—most of which are born out of an ending, an old era giving way to a new one. Our everyday lives are full of small-scale beginnings and endings—births, deaths, marriages. In BRF's 2007 Advent book, author Maggi Dawn reflects on six groups of people in the Bible; each provides a focus for the idea of beginnings and endings, and draws ancient wisdom from the human experience that happened in between. The following extracts are from Section 1: 'The Gospels and the salvation story'.

Early or late?

Read Psalm 27.

If you're reading this on the first of December, you may well already have had a Christmas card or two fall through your letter box. I love receiving Christmas cards, from the first ones that arrive on the first of December, to the ones that arrive with a slightly panicked message of lateness on Christmas Eve, to those that come with a sheepish apology around the third of January. Whenever they arrive, early or late, I'm always cheered up by this annual reminder of how many good friends I have.

I have to admit, though, that I find it slightly depressing that Christmas always seems to begin way ahead of schedule, when shop displays and Christmas lights go up in November or even earlier. So when the very first cards arrive on the first few days of December, I'm usually still feeling a bit 'bah-hum-buggy' about it all! But by the time the last posting day is upon us and I realise I'm behind schedule, then I envy the foresight of my early-bird friends and vow to be more like them next year! Certainly Christmas can sometimes feel less like a feast to be celebrated and more like a deadline to be reached. It's often, though not always, the woman in a household who carries the stress of everything being ready for Christmas, but Christmas creates deadlines for all sorts of other people too—church leaders, school teachers, retailers, and many others. Such moments focus very sharply your sense of time, and being bound by time.

In devotional terms, though,

following the seasons of the Church year can leave us with this feeling that things never happen at the right time. The realities of life rarely match up with the mood of the Church year—they always come too early or too late. If, as we travel through Lent or Advent, life is delivering abundant joys and happiness, the sombre tone of the season never quite hits home. But it's even harder to deal with if you are feeling down or low when Christmas or Easter arrives. A few years ago a friend and I wrote to each other all the way through Lent, sharing our reflections on the season. She was a great devotee of retreats and silent space; I was the mother of a newborn baby and silent spaces were few and far between. Our Lenten experience was quite profound that year, as we were both going through extreme lows for quite different reasons. On Easter Day my friend emailed to say, 'I'm so fed up with the Church year. Resurrection? I don't think so. I feel like I need to stay in Good Friday for a good long time yet.'

All too often we have this dislocated feeling of being out of time, out of step. And Christmas is a particularly difficult season to negotiate if you don't feel like celebrating. It's not only the Church, but the whole culture that feeds us an exaggerated image of happiness and celebration, which sets us up to feel very low if we are not in a party mood. Most of our life, though, is lived in this in-between place where things come early or late, but never on time.

Psalm 27 is sometimes given the title 'A Triumphant Song of Confidence'. I think it reads more like a defiant song than a triumphant one. The way the psalmist mixes up his tenses creates this interesting effect of reflecting on past promises fulfilled, asking for something to happen right now, stating that it's already happened, and confidently predicting that it will happen in the future. He seems at one and the same time to be giving thanks for something that is already here, and asking for help in the midst of trouble. There's an urgent anxiety about his cry for help: 'Do not cast me off, do not forsake me.' And perhaps there's even a touch of the childish promise to be good if God will only help him: 'Teach me your way O Lord, lead me on a level path.'

The psalmist's experience reminds me of the dislocation of our lives from the Church seasons. God's gifts do not always come according to our timetable, or at the moment when we think we need them. Advent and Christmas seem to promise us the presence of God, and yet it seems that some-

> *God's gifts do not always come according to our timetable*

times God hides his face and is nowhere to be found. But God's timetable is not the same as ours, and our sense of need or urgency doesn't twist God's arm into a response.

When I was a child, we had a maiden aunt, a remarkable and wonderful woman who always, absolutely dependably, forgot all our birthdays. But at some random time of year—May or July or November—a big parcel would arrive full of presents. They might say 'Happy Birthday' or 'Happy Christmas', regardless of the time of year. It seemed madly exciting to us to get a completely unexpected present just when life was going through a tedious moment. It was always books—she taught English literature, and was bang up to date on the latest releases—and they were always wonderful. The same aunt, when we went to stay, would sneak into our bedroom just before sunrise, pull jumpers over our pyjamas, and our bare feet into shoes with no socks (against mum's rules!), and quietly lead us out of the house, leaving everyone else asleep. Then she would pile my sister and me into her very old Austin and drive us down to the beach. This was in Somerset, where the beach goes out for about two miles at low tide. There she would actually drive across the sand—again, strictly against the rules, but there's no one there at sunrise to make you obey the rules—and out of the car would

appear a primus stove, an omelette pan, eggs, butter, salt, pepper, fresh bread… We ate omelettes and drank tea as the sun rose over the sea, and then went paddling in our pyjamas, breathing in great gulps of early morning salty air. The woman was a genius, and we adored her.

Whenever I forget a Christmas card, a birthday card or whatever, I think of Aunty Margaret. Please, God, let me be like her. I hope I never become the kind of person that demands diamonds and perfume on the right date. I hope I do become the kind of person who remembers to send gifts that someone will love, instead of gifts to satisfy a deadline. And whenever God's gifts elude me, when there is no joy at Easter, no wonder at Christmas, or simply no sense of God's presence in between times, again I think of Aunty Margaret. The gift will arrive at the right moment, even if not on the 'right' date. Joy on demand is joyless indeed, but omelettes on the beach and presents in July I can seriously live with.

If we confidently depend on the knowledge that God's gifts, unlike Santa's, are not delivered to a deadline, then we can live within the seasons knowing that the gift they represent will come to us, unexpectedly, not necessarily on time. We can say with hope, or even a little holy defiance, 'I believe that I shall see the goodness of the Lord in the land of the living.'

Luke: Let me tell you a story

Read Luke 1:1–7.

Luke's is the only one of the four Gospels to have this kind of Prologue, a little introductory statement as to why and how the Gospel was written. It's a matter of long debate whether Theophilus was the name of a real person, or whether the name, which means 'lover of God', was Luke's way of addressing his readers personally. Either way, the opening sentence has the effect of giving some sense of relationship between the story-teller and the reader. You get the sense that Luke is writing to you personally, not just addressing some nameless, faceless crowd.

Writing to real readers is one thing that makes Luke one of the best storytellers in the Bible. Another is the fact that he makes the people inside the story seem real too. Luke gives us more than historical plot, more than philosophy and doctrine: he gives us flesh-and-blood characters that we can identify with. In particular, he is the only one of the Gospel writers who brings Jesus' family to life. Matthew tells us about the surrounding circumstances of the birth stories, but only Luke has the 'inside' information. He said in his prologue that he had carefully investigated everything 'from the start'—the start of Jesus life, perhaps? It's possible that Luke may have known members of the Holy Family, and per-haps he even knew Mary, the mother of Jesus, in person. But he certainly had a source close to the family to get hold of these personal anecdotes.

Luke is a storyteller, but one with a respect for historical sense: he says he wants it to be an 'orderly' account. And his reason for telling the story is that he wants to pass on the faith. The words he uses in the Prologue are the words of a teacher: he speaks of what has been 'handed down', taught from one group to the next, and he speaks of the story as both 'truth' and 'instruction'. Luke, then, wants to give a rational and sensible account of the events that the Christian faith is based on, and he wants to tell them in such a way that it demands personal engage-ment with Jesus, not just rational assent to a belief system or obedi-ence to religious ritual.

Luke's Gospel, more than any other, tells the story of Jesus in the most humanly engaged way. Luke's characters climb off the pages and touch our heartstrings, not just our intellect. It's Luke who gave us the great emotive and personal stories of the Gospels—the parental agony and sibling rivalry of the prodigal son, the unexpected friendship of Jesus towards Zacchaeus, the weaving together of twelve years in the life of a woman and a girl, both of whom need new life, the confusion and pain of the disciples on the road to Emmaus. Luke declares his intent in the opening verses of his Gospel to give an account in the right order. The account he gives places things in time, and focuses the story on the impact of Jesus upon real people.

Luke's starting place is a focus on human interest, not on history or prophecy, but he deftly gives the story context and definition by highlighting the fact that it takes place in the context of history, politics and religion. 'In the days of King Herod of Judea, there was a priest,' he begins, and immediately tells us that the story starts in the temple in Jerusalem, the heart of first-century Judaism. It's a story about religious things but, as we shall see, a story that turns religious matters on their head. It's also a story that takes place in a political setting, in a nation under occupation, under the reign of a puppet king. That's important because the Gospel, as Luke tells it, has political consequences as well as religious ones. And he makes the story intensely personal by telling us that the priest and his wife 'were living righteously… but they had no children'. In Zechariah and Elizabeth's cultural context, to be childless was not only a personal grief but also an implied slight on their character, as childlessness carried a sense of divine judgement with it.

Luke begins, then, by telling us

> *Luke's starting place is a focus on human interest*

that the good news of Jesus happens at a moment in history to real people. He sets the scene for what will be disrupted and challenged and brought to account by the gospel, and for what will be rescued and salvaged and healed. He sets the good news of Jesus not merely in a religious setting but in the wider scheme of things. It's 'in the days of King Herod of Judea'—right in the midst of everyday life and political history, and Luke doesn't shy away from the fact that the gospel arrives in the midst of political injustice, in war zones and occupied territories, disrupting existing political and religious hierarchies. The good news is full of life and goodness, but it isn't well-behaved or polite. He also tells us that the good news is genuinely good news for real people—people who are faithful and good, but also people who are broken-hearted, for those whose hopes have been dashed, who live under a shadow because society unjustly hangs a question mark over their heads. Luke begins the good news, then, right in the heart of life: it will affect everything, political, religious, community and family. The gospel, for Luke, is not primarily conceptual. It's right here, right now, and it's thoroughly personal.

To order a copy of this book, please turn to the order form on page 159.

When You Walk

September 2007 sees the publication of a revised and expanded edition of *When You Walk*, a best-selling collection of *New Daylight* readings by Adrian Plass. Now with 365 readings, this book challenges us to explore the Bible honestly, expecting it to transform our relationship with God. Here is Adrian's introduction to twelve readings on art in the Bible, including dance, drama and architecture.

Landscapes of beauty

When this section came to mind, I felt quite excited. Some topics are so bursting with potential that it feels necessary only to plunge one's hands into the great treasure chest of scripture, scoop out armfuls of material, and then do just a little judicious editing. Occasionally it does happen a bit like that, but this time, for a long time, it did not. I simply was not able to think of a way into the theme, until, as is so often the case, I stopped thinking and did the most obvious and simple thing. I made a list. I listed all the different art forms that entered my head, from dance to dressmaking. Then I ran down the list once more, noting next to each item a place in the Bible where that particular skill or art is featured. I confess to drawing a blank on one or two, but I was amazed to discover the extent to which the arts are explicitly or implicitly mentioned in the Old and New Testaments.

I found this very invigorating. As we all know, there is a long and rich tradition of art and drama in the life of Christian communities. However, sections of the modern Church have passed through a phase of extreme wariness, especially towards artists who are unable to squeeze their productivity into the tight confines of a fear-shrunken religion. As a result, we have had to endure some Christian art that is reminiscent of those dreadful pictures from Communist Russia in which tractors seem to take centre stage. Thank God for those who have continued to follow their star as the wise men did, in order to arrive at the place where they were supposed to be, however odd the direction may have seemed. My prayer is that Christian artists will increase in numbers and confidence and be encouraged by the Bible. It rings with echoes of the wonderfully original work done by the greatest artist of all.

To order a copy of this book, please turn to the order form on page 159.

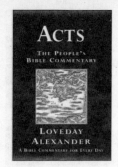

ACTS
THE PEOPLE'S
BIBLE COMMENTARY

LOVEDAY
ALEXANDER
A BIBLE COMMENTARY FOR EVERY DAY

The PBC:
a map for every journey

Naomi Starkey

While the publication date of *Acts*, the final volume in BRF's *People's Bible Commentary* series, is starting to recede into memory, the BRF team is still feeling delighted at completing this mammoth project. Stretching over more than a decade from first discussions to finish, the series provides accessible commentary on every book of the Bible, using a writing team from around the world and across the denominations.

So where does the PBC sit in relation to other commentary series? It's not exactly 'entry level', but it makes no claim to be the last scholarly word in detailed textual analysis. You don't need to understand Greek or Hebrew to use the PBC; neither does the series make Bible study a brain-numbingly dry exercise. These are devotional commentaries, which aim to provide food for thought, something to take away into the day, as well as gently building up your knowledge about the passage you have read.

But why use a commentary at all? Suppose you're on a tour of the country—by car or bike, or on foot. As you survey the landscape ahead of you, what do you see? Perhaps your route is a well-trodden path, full of picturesque views and well-known landmarks. Or you might have deliberately chosen unknown territory, hoping to discover hidden

beauty along the way. Maybe you're staring out over a stretch of ground that looks, to be honest, flat and uninspiring—or a range of hills that appears too daunting for your limited horsepower, tired muscles or inappropriate footwear.

Whatever your journey promises, a good map—or a set of them—is what you need to make the most of its challenges and delights. PBCs do that job for you as you explore the various books of the Bible. They help you cross the fast rivers, plunging valleys and rocky slopes of scripture, as well as the level paths through flowery meadows.

So what is the best way to use them? If we have enjoyed using one, how do we know which one to read next? Do we have to work our way consecutively through the Bible or is there a different approach?

In response to such questions, we have come up with four reading plans, using different selections of PBC volumes, to help you navigate your way across the Bible and get a sense of how it all fits together. Each plan is for a different kind of journey, each enabling you to make sense of varied terrain.

First of all, there is the 'Way in to the Bible' plan, an accessible approach that is ideal for those who previously may not have done more than dipped into the Bible. Beginning with Mark, the shortest Gospel, it covers some of the more familiar books of Old and New Testaments (Psalms 1—72, Genesis, Ephesians to Colossians, 1 and 2 Samuel, Psalms 73—150, Hosea to Micah) and ends with Romans, Paul's great letter clarifying the foundations of Christian belief.

Alternatively, we have the 'God's working in history' plan. This reading order gives a strong sense of God at work in individual lives, amid the clash of great and ancient empires. Starting with Luke, the fullest Gospel, it passes through Ruth, Esther, Acts, Chronicles to Nehemiah, 1 Corinthians, Jeremiah and 2 Corinthians. It concludes with Deuteronomy's powerful retelling of God's choosing of Israel as his people.

Our third plan, 'Roots of our faith', is based on the fact that the roots of the Christian faith are Jewish. The reading order traces that background, starting with Matthew's Gospel and continuing with the epic Exodus narrative. It then covers Galatians and 1 and 2 Thessalonians, 1 and 2 Kings, Isaiah and Timothy to Hebrews, followed by Nahum to Malachi. In a challenging conclusion, it covers Leviticus and Numbers, two books that can appear impenetrable but richly repay close and patient study.

The final plan is called 'God's mysterious wisdom'. It starts with John, the most enigmatic of the Gospels, and covers parts of scripture, ranging from the thought-provoking to the prophetic and visionary, that can be downright unsettling! Moving on from John, the plan covers Job, Joshua and Judges, James to Jude, Daniel, Proverbs, Ezekiel and finally the book of Revelation. While some of these texts may be hard going, they can all be understood (with the help of a good commentary) as pointing to the God who chooses to reveal himself to his creatures, while ultimately remaining beyond our understanding.

Four maps; four approaches: take your pick and choose your starting point. Exploring the Bible is a crucial part of the discipleship journey, and embarking on this adventure with the help of the PBC means that there is less chance of getting lost along the way!

Single PBC volumes are priced £7.99 or £8.99. Please turn to the order form on page 159 to buy the whole collection for only £175 (saving £92), all New Testament titles for £70 (save almost £40) or all Old Testament volumes for £105 (save over £50).

Barnabas RE Days

Lucy Moore

Being 'equipped for all terrain', for the *Barnabas* team, usually means either making sure the tread on the car tyres is up to scratch for a trek to a school in the far depths of Somerset, or checking that we've included the crucial hats, treasure chests, sheep and flippers (don't ask) needed for the various stories of the day. However, I guess it could also mean equipping children for some of the different situations they meet in life, through exciting exploration of the Bible during a *Barnabas* RE Day.

As you'll know, we're very proud of our unique work in schools, bringing the Bible to life through the creative arts, and these *Barnabas* RE Days keep going down well with children and teachers alike. We get some very encouraging comments from schools:

We all very much enjoyed our day with Martyn. We found him inspiring. I loved the creation story he told my Reception class. It gave me many ideas for follow-up work. Martyn's assembly was thought-provoking and involved the whole school. We feel very privileged to have shared a day with him.

PAIVI PAYNE, CHRIST CHURCH CE PRIMARY SCHOOL, GREENWICH

It was great to have Lucy with us for the day. She brought the Bible to life in assembly and in the workshops. The children loved her enthusiasm,

fun and good ideas. We all had a different super day.

CHERYL SUTCLIFFE, MARSTON THOROLD'S CHARITY CE SCHOOL, GRANTHAM

John was very amenable and good with all the children. All staff felt the day was valuable and that the children got a lot from it. We all had a great day, thanks to all.

VAL RENOWDEN, LITTLE BLOXWICH CE VC PRIMARY SCHOOL, WALSALL

In 2006, after much team discussion, bringing together our joint experience of what works well in schools and of appropriate approaches to the Bible when working with children, we introduced a new theme to our range for *Barnabas* RE Days and started offering 'What's so special about the Bible?' to schools. Some teachers feel ill-equipped to tackle the huge questions about the Bible that are posed both by RE schemes of work and by the children themselves, so it seemed that this is another area where *Barnabas* can bring expertise to add value to the RE in a school.

I had my first attempt at the new material in a Catholic girls' school in Reading. We had a fascinating time and the girls threw themselves with great enthusiasm into various exploratory activities to do with images of the Bible, brought the story of Philip and the Ethiopian to life most dramatically and particularly relished the chance to see the bigger picture of the Bible rolled out before them. Martyn spent a day with a school in Towcester on the same theme. His report gives you a good idea of the range of activities covered, and the welcome questioning attitude of the children.

After lunch the topic changed. The sessions with Years 5 and 6 focused on the Bible itself and why it is such a special book. Once again some simple activities and drama games introduced the range and scope of the books in the Bible, the different writers and how the Bible describes itself. For the latter, the children threw themselves into creating statues that represented similes such as light, a sword, honey and a treasure chest. There were some imaginative ideas ranging from beehives to long-life

> *You can buy Barnabas gift vouchers for a school*

bulbs. Time and space (we were in the music room) meant we never got to explore any particular episode in depth but we did end each session with another reflective story, which we have called 'the story of the Story'. This tries to present how the Bible came together as the book that we know today, from the oral tradition around a campfire, via the Ten Commandments, the Torah, various scrolls of the prophets, parchments and manuscripts to the printed book. This prompted much discussion, including requests that I try to translate the Latin on the illuminated manuscript and interpret the marks on the clay tablets!

Barnabas RE Days are reaching children across the UK with insights about and from the Bible in a huge way. Perhaps this exciting ministry is something you could help to bring to a school near you? The *Barnabas* voucher scheme enables you to do just that. You can buy *Barnabas* gift vouchers for a school that can be used either towards our resources or towards the cost of a *Barnabas* RE Day. For full details, ring the *Barnabas* administrator on 01865 319704 or see our website: www.barnabasinchurches.org.uk.

Lucy Moore is an author, actor and storyteller, using her gifts as a member of the Barnabas *Ministry team.*

Guidelines © BRF 2007

The Bible Reading Fellowship
First Floor, Elsfield Hall, 15–17 Elsfield Way, Oxford OX2 8FG
Tel: 01865 319700; Fax: 01865 319701
E-mail: enquiries@brf.org.uk
Website: www.brf.org.uk

ISBN 978 1 84101 383 1

Distributed in Australia by:
Willow Connection, PO Box 288, Brookvale, NSW 2100.
Tel: 02 9948 3957; Fax: 02 9948 8153;
E-mail: info@willowconnection.com.au
Available also from all good Christian bookshops in Australia.
For individual and group subscriptions in Australia:
Mrs Rosemary Morrall, PO Box W35, Wanniassa, ACT 2903.

Distributed in New Zealand by:
Scripture Union Wholesale, PO Box 760, Wellington
Tel: 04 385 0421; Fax: 04 384 3990; E-mail: suwholesale@clear.net.nz

Distributed in Canada by:
The Anglican Book Centre, 80 Hayden Street, Toronto, Ontario, M4Y 3G2
Tel: 001 416 924-1332; Fax: 001 416 924-2760;
E-mail: abc@anglicanbookcentre.com; Website: www.anglicanbookcentre.com

Publications distributed to more than 60 countries

Acknowledgments

The New Revised Standard Version of the Bible, Anglicized Edition, copyright © 1989, 1995 by the Division of Christian Education of the National Council of the Churches of Christ in the USA. Used by permission. All rights reserved.

The Revised Standard Version of the Bible, copyright © 1946, 1952, 1971 by the Division of Christian Education of the National Council of the Churches of Christ in the United States of America. Used by permission. All rights reserved.

The Holy Bible, New International Version, copyright © 1973, 1978, 1984 by International Bible Society. Used by permission of Hodder & Stoughton, a division of Hodder Headline Ltd. All rights reserved. 'NIV' is a registered trademark of International Bible Society. UK trademark number 1448790.

Extracts from the Authorized Version of the Bible (The King James Bible), the rights in which are vested in the Crown, are reproduced by permission of the Crown's Patentee, Cambridge University Press.

New English Bible copyright © 1961, 1970 by Oxford University Press and Cambridge University Press.

Extracts from the New Jerusalem Bible, published and copyright © 1985 by Darton, Longman and Todd Ltd and les Editions du Cerf, and by Doubleday, a division of Bantam Doubleday Dell Publishing Group, Inc. Used by permission of Darton, Longman and Todd Ltd, and Doubleday, a division of Random House, Inc.

New American Standard Bible copyright © 1960, 1962, 1963, 1968, 1971, 1972, 1973, 1975, 1977, 1995 by The Lockman Foundation.

Printed in Singapore by Craft Print International Ltd

BRF is a Christian charity committed to resourcing the spiritual journey of adults and children alike. For adults, BRF publishes Bible reading notes and books and offers an annual programme of quiet days and retreats. Under its children's imprint *Barnabas*, BRF publishes a wide range of books for those working with children under 11 in school, church and home. BRF's *Barnabas Ministry* team offers INSET sessions for primary teachers, training for children's leaders in church, quiet days, and a range of events to enable children themselves to engage with the Bible and its message.

We need your help if we are to make a real impact on the local church and community. In an increasingly secular world people need even more help with their Bible reading, their prayer and their discipleship. We can do something about this, but our resources are limited. With your help, if we all do a little, together we can make a huge difference.

How can you help?

• You could support BRF's ministry with a donation or standing order (using the response form overleaf).

• You could consider making a bequest to BRF in your will, and so give lasting support to our work. (We have a leaflet available with more information about this, which can be requested using the form overleaf.)

• And, most important of all, you could support BRF with your prayers.

Whatever you can do or give, we thank you for your support.

BRF – resourcing your spiritual journey

BRF MINISTRY APPEAL RESPONSE FORM

Name _____

Address _____

_____ Postcode _____

Telephone _____ Email _____

(tick as appropriate)

Gift Aid Declaration

☐ I am a UK taxpayer. I want BRF to treat as Gift Aid Donations all donations I make from 6 April 2000 until I notify you otherwise.

Signature _____ Date _____

☐ I would like to support BRF's ministry with a regular donation by standing order (please complete the Banker's Order below).

Standing Order – Banker's Order

To the Manager, Name of Bank/Building Society _____

Address _____

_____ Postcode _____

Sort Code _____ Account Name _____

Account No _____

Please pay Royal Bank of Scotland plc, Drummonds, 49 Charing Cross, London SW1A 2DX (Sort Code 16-00-38), for the account of BRF A/C No. 00774151

The sum of _____ pounds on ___ / ___ / ___ (insert date your standing order starts) and thereafter the same amount on the same day of each month until further notice.

Signature _____ Date _____

Single donation .

☐ I enclose my cheque/credit card/Switch card details for a donation of

£5 £10 £25 £50 £100 £250 (other) £ _____ to support BRF's ministry

Credit/Switch card no. ☐☐☐☐☐☐☐☐☐☐☐☐☐☐☐☐☐☐☐

Expires ☐☐☐☐ Security code ☐☐☐ Issue no. of Switch card ☐☐☐☐

Signature _____ Date _____

(Where appropriate, on receipt of your donation, we will send you a Gift Aid form)

☐ Please send me information about making a bequest to BRF in my will.

Please detach and send this completed form to: Richard Fisher, BRF, First Floor, Elsfield Hall, 15–17 Elsfield Way, Oxford OX2 8FG. BRF is a Registered Charity (No.233280)

GL0307

BIBLE READING RESOURCES PACK

A pack of resources and ideas to help to promote Bible reading in your church is available from BRF. The pack, which will be of use at any time during the year, includes sample editions of the notes, magazine articles, leaflets about BRF Bible reading resources and much more. Unless you specify the month in which you would like the pack sent, we will send it immediately on receipt of your order. We greatly appreciate your donations towards the cost of producing the pack (without them we would not be able to make the pack available) and we welcome your comments about the contents of the pack and your ideas for future ones.

This coupon should be sent to:

BRF
First Floor
Elsfield Hall
15–17 Elsfield Way
Oxford
OX2 8FG

Name ————————————————————————

Address ————————————————————————

————————————————————————————————

———————————————————— Postcode ——————————

Telephone ————————————————————

Email ————————————————————————————

Please send me ———— Bible Reading Resources Pack(s)

Please send the pack now/ in ———————————— (month).

I enclose a donation for £ ———— towards the cost of the pack.

BRF is a Registered Charity

❏ Please send me a Bible reading resources pack to encourage Bible reading in my church

❏ I would like to take out a subscription myself (complete your name and address details only once)

❏ I would like to give a gift subscription (please complete both name and address sections below)

Your name _____

Your address _____

_____ Postcode _____

Gift subscription name _____

Gift subscription address _____

_____ Postcode _____

Please send *Guidelines* beginning with the January / May / September 2008 issue: (delete as applicable)

(please tick box)	UK	SURFACE	AIR MAIL
GUIDELINES	❏ £12.75	❏ £14.10	❏ £16.35
GUIDELINES 3-year sub	❏ £30.00		

I would like to take out an annual subscription to *Quiet Spaces* beginning with the next available issue:

(please tick box)	UK	SURFACE	AIR MAIL
QUIET SPACES	❏ £16.95	❏ £18.45	❏ £20.85

Please complete the payment details below and send your coupon, with appropriate payment, to: **BRF, First Floor, Elsfield Hall, 15–17 Elsfield Way, Oxford OX2 8FG.**

Total enclosed £ _____ (cheques should be made payable to 'BRF')

Payment by cheque ❏ postal order ❏ Visa ❏ Mastercard ❏ Switch ❏

Card number: ☐☐☐☐☐☐☐☐☐☐☐☐☐☐☐☐

Expires: ☐☐☐☐ Security code ☐☐☐ Issue no (Switch): ☐☐☐☐

Signature (essential if paying by credit/Switch card) _____

BRF is a Registered Charity

BRF PUBLICATIONS ORDER FORM

Please ensure that you complete and send off both sides of this order form.

Please send me the following book(s):

		Quantity	Price	Total
497 5	Meeting the Saviour (D. Tidball)	_____	£6.99	_____
535 4	An Emergent Theology for Emerging Churches (R. Anderson)	_____	£8.99	_____
566 8	Beginnings and Endings (M. Dawn)	_____	£7.99	_____
214 8	The Promise of Christmas (F. Dorrell)	_____	£4.99	_____
526 2	The Barnabas Children's Bible (R. Davies)	_____	£12.99	_____
531 6	When You Walk (new edn) (A. Plass)	_____	£12.99	_____
439 5	Caring for Creation (ed. S. Tillett)	_____	£8.99	_____
314 5	PBC: Genesis (G. West)	_____	£8.99	_____
095 3	PBC: Joshua and Judges (S.D. Mathewson)	_____	£7.99	_____
070 0	PBC: Chronicles to Nehemiah (M. Tunnicliffe)	_____	£7.99	_____
094 6	PBC: Job (K. Dell)	_____	£7.99	_____
031 1	PBC: Psalms 1—72 (D. Coggan)	_____	£8.99	_____
065 6	PBC: Psalms 73–150 (D. Coggan)	_____	£7.99	_____
245 2	PBC: Hosea to Micah (P. Gooder)	_____	£8.99	_____
028 1	PBC: Nahum to Malachi (G. Emmerson)	_____	£7.99	_____
191 2	PBC: Matthew (J. Proctor)	_____	£8.99	_____
046 5	PBC: Mark (D. France)	_____	£8.99	_____
027 4	PBC: Luke (H. Wansbrough)	_____	£7.99	_____
029 8	PBC: John (R.A. Burridge)	_____	£8.99	_____
216 2	PBC: Acts (L. Alexander)	_____	£8.99	_____
082 3	PBC: Romans (J.D.G. Dunn)	_____	£8.99	_____
122 6	PBC: 1 Corinthians (J. Murphy O'Connor)	_____	£7.99	_____
073 1	PBC: 2 Corinthians (A. Besancon Spencer)	_____	£7.99	_____
047 2	PBC: Ephesians to Colossians and Philemon (M. Maxwell)	_____	£7.99	_____
363 3	PBC: Revelation (M. Maxwell)	_____	£8.99	_____
	PBC: Entire collection (32 volumes)	_____	£175.00	_____
	PBC: All New Testament volumes	_____	£70.00	_____
	PBC: All Old Testament volumes	_____	£105.00	_____

Total cost of books £ _____

Donation £ _____

Postage and packing £ _____

TOTAL £ _____

POSTAGE AND PACKING CHARGES

order value	UK	Europe	Surface	Air Mail
£7.00 & under	£1.25	£3.00	£3.50	£5.50
£7.01–£30.00	£2.25	£5.50	£6.50	£10.00
Over £30.00	free	prices on request		

See over for payment details. All prices are correct at time of going to press, are subject to the prevailing rate of VAT and may be subject to change without prior warning.

PAYMENT DETAILS

Please complete the payment details below and send with appropriate payment and completed order form to:

**BRF, First Floor, Elsfield Hall,
15–17 Elsfield Way, Oxford OX2 8FG**

Name _____

Address _____

_____

_____ Postcode _____

Telephone _____

Email _____

Total enclosed £ _____(cheques should be made payable to 'BRF')

Payment by cheque ❏ postal order ❏ Visa ❏ Mastercard ❏ Switch ❏

Card number: ☐☐☐☐☐☐☐☐☐☐☐☐☐☐☐☐☐☐☐

Expires: ☐☐☐☐ Security code ☐☐☐ Issue no (Switch): ☐☐☐☐

Signature (essential if paying by credit/Switch card)_____

❏ Please do not send me further information about BRF publications.

ALTERNATIVE WAYS TO ORDER

Christian bookshops: All good Christian bookshops stock BRF publications. For your nearest stockist, please contact BRF.

Telephone: The BRF office is open between 09.15 and 17.30.
To place your order, phone 01865 319700; fax 01865 319701.

Website: Visit www.brf.org.uk

BRF is a Registered Charity

GL0307